MATTHEW
A Devotional Commentary

Meditations on the Gospel According to St. Matthew

GENERAL EDITOR
Leo Zanchettin

The Word Among Us
9639 Doctor Perry Road
Ijamsville, Maryland 21754
www.wau.org
ISBN: 0-932085-12-1

Scripture quotations are from the Revised Standard Version of the
Bible, copyright 1946, 1952, 1971, by the Division of Christian
Education of the National Council of the Churches of Christ in the
U.S.A. Used by permission.

Cover art: Caravaggio (1573-1610) S. Matteo e l'Angelo/Art Resource, NY
Cover design by David Crosson

Made and printed in the United States of America.

Foreword

Dear Friends in Christ:

At one point in his gospel, Matthew tells how Jesus exclaimed: "I thank you, Father, Lord of heaven and earth, that you have hidden these things from the wise and understanding and revealed them to babes" (Matthew 11:25). Jesus knew that God delighted in revealing his love and his plan to the humble and simple of heart. It was in the same sense that we set out to produce this devotional commentary on the Gospel of Matthew. While we can learn much through scholarly research, our primary goal for this commentary is that it would help people meet Jesus in prayer.

Because of this goal, the following commentary does not set out to answer all the questions that scripture scholars have studied and debated over the centuries. More than anything else, we want to encourage lay Catholics to open the scriptures and listen to the Holy Spirit speaking the word of God to the human heart. Every passage of Matthew's gospel contains its own hidden treasures, and it is in prayer that we can discover these treasures for ourselves.

We want to thank every one of those at *The Word Among Us* who have made this commentary possible. Many of the meditations in this commentary were initially developed for *The Word*

Among Us monthly publication, and we want to thank all of the writers of these meditations for granting us permission to reprint their work. In addition, we want to thank Fr. Joseph Mindling, O.F.M. Cap., Mrs. Patricia Mitchell, Mr. Gregory Roa, and Mrs. Theresa Keller for their contributions.

Finally, we want to dedicate this work to the Lord Jesus Christ who taught us in the Beatitudes (Matthew 5:3-12) not only how to live, but how he himself lived as he walked among us. May his grace extend to all of us as we seek to be conformed more and more to his image.

Leo Zanchettin
General Editor

Table of Contents

An Introduction to Matthew's Gospel

Fr. Joseph A. Mindling, O.F.M. Cap.

Wouldn't it be exciting if we could have a personal conversation with the authors who first captured the words and deeds of Jesus in the gospels of the New Testament? Perhaps we would come to such an interview with a list of questions that have piqued our curiosity for a long time. Or maybe we would just ask these writers to read the inspired texts out loud for us, adding an explanatory remark here and there.

The "Fountain" of Scripture

What could we hope to gain from such an exchange? Some might come with nothing more than a desire to be entertained, like Herod Antipas who tried to impress his courtiers by getting Jesus to perform a miracle. Most people who already love and admire our Lord would be deeply pleased if they could simply learn something more about him. It surely would be enriching to discover new information about the world in which Jesus lived and worked. But the best thing of all would be to learn more about our Friend and Savior as a Person.

As far as we know, the four witnesses whose names have become shorthand titles for the gospels are not granting interviews like this in our day. And yet, what we might dream of obtaining from such a dialogue may be more accessible to us than we normally think. The Vatican II document on divine revelation tells us that the scriptures are like a "fountain." This image of a gushing source of clear water reminds us that the inspired Word of God in the Bible has something new and refreshing for us no matter how many times we dip back into it.

Jesus promised that the Father would send the Spirit, the Paraclete, to teach us and help us understand more profoundly what he had taught. "I have much more to tell you, but you cannot bear it now. When he comes, though, the Spirit of truth will guide you to all truth" (see John 14:17; 15:26; 16:13). When we approach the gospels with an eagerness to receive this truth, we can actually do more than have a dialogue with an evangelist. With the guidance of the Spirit, we can pass from reading *about* Jesus to a new level of communication *with* Jesus. Even nonbelievers often find the gospel records of our Lord's life quite interesting, but to those who come with "faith seeking understanding," the reverent reading of the text becomes a place where we find Jesus, and where Jesus finds us.

Unity in Diversity

The present commentary has been written to help us meet the Messiah in the pages of the Gospel according to Matthew. In modern translations of the Bible, this is the first book of the New Testament, an account that starts by looking at some of the people and events connected with Jesus' birth, moves into a description of his work and teaching as an adult, and climaxes with the account of his death and resurrection. Since this sequence sounds similar to the narratives in all the gospels, it might be useful to ask an obvious question here: Why not dovetail the various stories, fitting together what is unique in each of the four around the "core" that they share? Why not write our reflections based on a hybrid, homogenized "life" of Christ?

This suggestion was already taken up by the middle of the second century with the composition of what early church historians know as the *Diatessaron*. Yet even though such "gospel harmonies" (as they are called in English) were available, the Christian people opted overwhelmingly for the continued private and liturgical use of the individual inspired accounts. Modern scripture scholars, still busily rediscovering fascinating editorial nuances in all four of them, can only applaud the ancient preservation of this wonderful unity in diversity. Hopefully, our close examination and prayerful savoring of each canonical gospel will make this even more obvious.

None of the gospels provides us with a detailed account of Jesus' entire earthly life and, unlike many modern biographers, the evangelists do not focus heavily on a "psychological" picture of our Lord. The church has always insisted on the solidly historical character of the words and deeds reported in the gospels, but it is obvious that first-generation Christians knew much more about Jesus than has been preserved in the New Testament. The Fourth Gospel ends with an explicit acknowledgment of this:

> There are also many other things which Jesus did; were every one of them to be written, I suppose that the world itself could not contain the books that would be written. (John 21:25)

On what grounds, then, did the gospel writers decide to include, combine, or omit particular details or episodes? The indications that can be drawn from the finished products—the gospels themselves—point primarily to pastoral concerns. The evangelists wrote above all to persuade their readers to accept Jesus in faith, to learn more about him, and to let him continue to act and speak through these records of his earthly mission. To respond to these texts in the spirit in which they were written, we today need to approach them not as encyclopedia articles, but as invitations to deepen our own understanding and our personal commitment.

Matthew's Gospel

Christian tradition has called the first book in the New Testament the "Gospel of Matthew," or, simply, "Matthew." The official name of this work, "the Gospel *according to* Matthew"— which we still use in the liturgy today—reminds us that the early church was much less focused on the literary task of individual authors than on their connections with the original witnesses of the Good News. The oldest testimonies about this gospel identify Matthew with the tax collector whose calling we read about in Matthew 9:9-13 and 10:3. Unfortunately, these precious few verses tell us little that is distinctive about this apostle, and they throw no light on what the words "according to" might have conveyed to ancient readers. On the other hand, what the gospel itself reveals about the community for which it was written can help modern readers enter Matthew's circle of believers and discover what they need to learn about Jesus.

Educated estimates put the composition date around 80-85 A.D., a time when relations between the church and the synagogue were reaching the breaking point. The way modern Christians and Jews take for granted their almost total religious separation was not the situation among the readers that Matthew had primarily in mind. Many of the first converts to Christianity worked zealously to attract other Jewish individuals and families to the Way of the Nazarene. At the same time, those who rejected Jesus made concerted efforts to denigrate his name, intimidating would-be followers with threats of persecution and expulsion from the religious communities where many of them had been raised. The Gospel of

Matthew was forged in the heated altercations and sometimes even physical violence that accompanied this fierce competition.

Meeting Jesus Through Matthew

Although the public polemics have subsided, many of the issues that concerned the early church have never lost their radical religious importance, despite the dramatic differences between first-century Palestine and our world today. Let us consider three questions that figure prominently throughout this gospel and begin to reflect on how they might lead us to a more personal contact with Jesus and his teachings in our situation as Christians now.

One of the central preoccupations of the first gospel is the need to understand Jesus as the crowning fulfillment of an initiative God had taken centuries earlier with the patriarchal families whose stories are preserved in the book of Genesis. For Matthew, as for us, this was not some theoretical debate or a question about historical trivia. If Jesus was not the Messiah he claimed to be, then either he was a charlatan, or the God of the Covenant had finally abandoned the relationship he had promised to maintain forever with the descendants of Abraham and Sarah. The more than forty Old Testament quotes that permeate this gospel never let the reader forget that Jesus was not a last-minute "substitute" for a divine design that had floundered under the weight of human infidelity. Since God had both foreseen and brought about the Christ event, these quotations point to a loving providence that remains constantly faithful throughout the ages to those who accept Jesus as the promised Messiah.

A closely related theme which also figures prominently in this gospel is its vision of individual Christian believers interacting as a community assembled by God's initiative. Many pagans in the first century worked on the premise that religion was essentially a human undertaking, an approach aimed at bribing or placating the forces of nature. Jesus assured us, on the contrary, that "you did not choose me, but I chose you" (John 15:16). The special term *ek-klesia* which Matthew uses to express the idea of "church" preserves the emphasis on this divine initiative because in Greek it means "those called forth." The Old Testament had already adopted this terminology to highlight the status of Israel as God's special people. Its continued use in the New Testament is based on the conviction that Jesus has extended membership in this family of faith to all who accept his call. Praying along with the Gospel of Matthew will remind us repeatedly about God's unflagging interest in how we live and worship and work together with these brothers and sisters. Being "church" means forgiving and being forgiven, seeking the face of Christ among our brothers and sisters, and rediscovering them as our family when we find ourselves really at home with him.

A third set of ideas that stand out in the first gospel concerns the question of how we grow in our ability to please God and in our understanding of what it means to pray, "Your kingdom come, Your will be done." A major challenge for the earliest converts from Judaism to Christianity was the discernment of how their religious heritage should be retained and at the same time made new in Christ. The Sermon on the Mount and various other passages throughout this gospel insist on the preservation of the Old Testament and counsel a respect for religious leaders, yet Jesus does not speak simply of a blind obedience but of a "fulfillment" of the law. As we open ourselves to his teaching, we hope to enter into the spirit of the commandments, moving beyond the "letter" to grasp the way our love for God and for one another is supposed to shape all that we do.

One way to react to this theme might be to consider it an interesting but ancient problem, a difficulty for the first generations of the church, but now of little more than historical interest.

In fact, however, all of us are called on to "outgrow" the earlier stages of our faith and its imperfect manifestations. Praying with this gospel can help us identify the areas of our lives where our fervor has diminished or where we hear ourselves being called to a more intense and a more spiritually motivated approach to life.

Like the other gospels, Matthew recounts the time of Jesus' public life in the form of relatively short episodes that always include important sayings and teachings. Those who study this writing from an academic standpoint often point to a broad-stroked rhythm, an alteration between sections that focus more on Jesus' encounters with individuals and those that present his lengthier discourses, especially these five: The Sermon on the Mount (Matthew 5:1–7:29), The Missionary Sermon (10:5-42), The Seven Parables about the Kingdom (13:1-52), The Sermon about Church Life (18:1-35), and the Sermon about the End Times (24:1–25:46). Sometimes it is helpful to watch for these passages, or to keep track of the increasing hostility Jesus encountered among the religious and political leaders as he revealed more about his mission and his identity. At other times, we can simply "go with the flow" and let the Spirit guide the reading and reflection that will raise our hearts and minds.

He Speaks to Our Hearts

The Vatican II document on divine revelation mentioned above closes with an exhortation to accompany all of our scripture reading with prayer. This is welcome advice, but we must remember that prayer is a two-way communication.

An interesting illustration of this fact took place several years ago when a representative from the International Bible Society went to interview the leader of a tribal group in the mountains of Central America. After years of listening to Spanish translations of the New Testament, the people in this area had finally been able to hear the words of the gospels in their own language, a Mayan dialect used by relatively few people. When the visiting scholar questioned the chief about the experience of hearing the words of Jesus in his own tongue, it prompted a thought-provoking reply. "It is wonderful," the man said, "but now Jesus is always telling me what to do."

In a certain sense, this is what happens to all of us when we go to the scriptures and speak to the Jesus we find there. He does more than listen. He speaks to our hearts.

Scripture: A Conversation With God

By Theresa Keller and Leo Zanchettin

In the sacred books, the Father who is in heaven comes lovingly to meet his children, and talks with them. (Vatican II: Dogmatic Constitution on Divine Revelation, *21*)

What could be a greater honor than having a conversation with Almighty God, the Creator of everything that exists? Wouldn't it be wonderful to be able to know what is in his heart and to understand his intentions and desires? As the Fathers of the Second Vatican Council pointed out, we have this opportunity every time we open the Bible. Scripture is not simply a collection of words to be read, however wise or moving these words may be. Scripture is the word of God—his voice speaking intimately to us, refreshing us and teaching us. In scripture, God opens his heart and shares his thoughts with his children, bestowing on them a high dignity as he forms them after his very own likeness.

The challenge we often face in reading scripture is to allow the words on the page to have an impact on our hearts. Imagine a young boy whose conversations with his father go far beyond simple facts and duties. He feels free to share his accomplishments and failures with him and knows his father will always listen and help him. He knows his father understands the boy's hopes and fears, his dreams and plans. The father *knows* his son and is happily working with him to help him grow into a strong, loving, and responsible man. In a similar way, God our Father longs to teach us and form us, and he does this as we open our hearts to his word.

Lectio Divina—Reading the Scriptures in Faith

Tradition provides a way of reading scripture, known as *lectio divina*, or *inspired reading*, in which God's word can change our hearts. In its truest sense, *lectio divina* is meant to draw us from the word of God in scripture to God the Word—Jesus himself, who gives us a share in his wisdom and love. *Lectio divina* involves four steps: reading, meditation, prayer, and contemplation. Guigo the Carthusian, a spiritual writer from the Middle Ages, described these steps in the following way:

> Reading is the careful study of the Scriptures, concentrating all one's powers on it. Meditation is the busy application of the mind to seek, with the help of one's own reason, for knowledge of hidden truth. Prayer is the heart's devoted turning to God to drive away evil and obtain what is good. Contemplation is when the mind is in some sort lifted up to God and held above itself, so that it tastes the joys of everlasting sweetness. . . . Seek in reading and you will find in meditating; knock in mental prayer and it will be opened to you by contemplation (see *Catechism of the Catholic Church*, 2654).

Reading and Meditation: The Words of Scripture

Reading and *meditation* primarily focus on the actual words of scripture and their meaning. The stage called *reading* involves reading a passage of scripture and understanding what it says. Read the passage carefully a couple of times. Try reading it aloud as well, paying attention to the way the words should be spoken. You may want to outline the main points of the passage, or try to put them into your own words. Who is speaking to whom? Why? What are the main events or facts being communicated? What is the context of the passage? What situation gave rise to these words? Resources such as commentaries, Bible dictionaries, or other study guides can help uncover more dimensions of the rich tapestry that is God's word. The challenge in this stage is to remain focused on the words themselves, even if we are referencing other works *about* the word of God.

In *meditation* we move beyond what the passage *says* to try to uncover what it *means*. We move from the *then* of history to the *now* of our lives. In this stage, it's good to focus on one particular part of the passage—a word or a phrase that has struck us—and ponder that part quietly and peacefully. Begin to open your mind to the Spirit and the heavenly dimension of the words. Let the word speak to your own situation, to challenge you or to comfort you, to move you to repentance or to praise and worship. In meditation, the immediate words we have read give way to the timeless truths of the gospel that give us life.

Prayer and Contemplation: The Word in Our Hearts

The wonderful promise of studying scripture is that our study does not end with the efforts of our human intellect alone. In *prayer* and *contemplation*, the focus moves from the words of God to Jesus himself. God's word is not only the written word in scripture, but the very Person of Jesus, the Word made flesh (John 1:14).

In *prayer* we respond to the word of God, asking the Spirit to write these words on our hearts. As God's children, we have freedom to pray simply and spontaneously, whether that means singing, asking God questions, or just worshipping him for his goodness and perfection. We can confess our sins to the Lord and ask him to give us the grace to live in greater faithfulness to his word. It is in prayer that we begin a heartfelt conversation with God our heavenly Father. As the Fathers of the Second Vatican Council wrote: "Prayer should accompany the reading of Sacred Scripture, so that a dialogue takes place between God and man. For 'we speak to him when we pray; we listen to him when we read the divine oracles' " (*Dogmatic Constitution on Divine Revelation*, 25).

In *contemplation*, we quiet our hearts in Jesus' presence and allow him to touch us, heal us, and move us. Having gone through the door of scripture, we are now in the chamber of the Lord who is our King and Friend. In contemplation, we gaze upon his beauty and his glory and receive from him the grace and strength to live out the words we have read and meditated upon. Like the two disciples on the road to Emmaus, our hearts can burn with love for God as Jesus opens the scriptures to us (Luke 24:13-32). God knows exactly what we need, and through contemplation, we can stay with him a while and be encouraged and strengthened by him.

Living in the Word

In scripture, God has set a table of the choicest food for our souls. How can we respond to his invitation to come and eat with him? Very practically, it is important that we plan a specific time of the day when we can devote our full attention to his word. We are more likely to protect a set time for reading and prayer rather than waiting for some "free time" that may never come along. It is also good to choose a place that is quiet and free from distractions, a private place where we feel comfortable and peaceful.

How can we prepare our hearts to hear the Lord? Before we begin reading, we can take a moment to recall the truths of our faith: God created us out of love; through baptism into Jesus' death and resurrection, we can receive forgiveness and freedom; we are all invited to know him personally through the indwelling Holy Spirit; the church is his beloved bride, the gathering of his people; Jesus will return at the end of time as Judge and Redeemer. Establishing these truths at the start can put our minds at rest and give us confidence that God does want to speak to us.

How should we decide what passage to read on a given day? You might try reading through a specific book of the Bible, like Exodus or 1 Corinthians. You may instead decide to follow a certain biblical theme, such as love, justice, or the kingdom of God. Another way is to follow the church's liturgical calendar, keeping in touch with the daily Mass readings. Whichever way you choose, make sure you are open to the Spirit's power to bring the words to life in your heart.

Once we have spent our time with God's word, it is wise to write out what we have learned. This will not only help us remember the word better, but it will enable us to look back over time and see how God has taught us step by step. As the Lord's truths and his character are imprinted on our hearts, we will have a great treasure house from which we can draw at any time as we face the temptations and challenges of our daily lives.

God enjoys sharing his heart with us. He created us to be as intimate with him as children are with their parents, and as a bride is with her husband. Every day, he asks us to spend time with him and receive the word of life. As we open ourselves to his word, we allow God to refresh us by writing his truth on our hearts. Every time we pick up scripture, we can ask the Holy Spirit to teach us how to read the word that he has given us.

The Beginnings

MATTHEW
1–4

Matthew 1:1-17

1 The book of the genealogy of Jesus Christ, the son of David, the son of Abraham.

2 Abraham was the father of Isaac, and Isaac the father of Jacob, and Jacob the father of Judah and his brothers, 3 and Judah the father of Perez and Zerah by Tamar, and Perez the father of Hezron, and Hezron the father of Ram, 4 and Ram the father of Amminadab, and Amminadab the father of Nahshon, and Nahshon the father of Salmon, 5 and Salmon the father of Boaz by Rahab, and Boaz the father of Obed by Ruth, and Obed the father of Jesse, 6 and Jesse the father of David the king.

And David was the father of Solomon by the wife of Uriah, 7 and Solomon the father of Rehoboam, and Rehoboam the father of Abijah, and Abijah the father of Asa, 8 and Asa the father of Jehoshaphat, and Jehoshaphat the father of Joram, and Joram the father of Uzziah, 9 and Uzziah the father of Jotham, and Jotham the father of Ahaz, and Ahaz the father of Hezekiah, 10 and Hezekiah the father of Manasseh, and Manasseh the father of Amos, and Amos the father of Josiah, 11 and Josiah the father of Jechoniah and his brothers, at the time of the deportation to Babylon.

12 And after the deportation to Babylon: Jechoniah was the father of Shealtiel, and Shealtiel the father of Zerubbabel, 13 and Zerubbabel the father of Abiud, and Abiud the father of Eliakim, and Eliakim the father of Azor, 14 and Azor the father of Zadok, and Zadok the father of Achim, and Achim the father of Eliud, 15 and Eliud the father of Eleazar, and Eleazar the father of Matthan, and Matthan the father of Jacob, 16 and Jacob the father of Joseph the husband of Mary, of whom Jesus was born, who is called Christ.

17 So all the generations from Abraham to David were fourteen generations, and from David to the deportation to Babylon fourteen generations, and from the deportation to Babylon to the Christ fourteen generations.

The listing of Jesus' genealogy at the beginning of Matthew's gospel may seem tedious to the modern mind, yet it does establish Jesus' place in the Jewish tradition and his continuity with the great figures of the Old Testament. One can also see in it the long and deliberate preparation by the Father for the sending of the Son. God's plan was developed carefully and made use of the material at hand—some admirable people and some who were not so perfect.

Bible scholars have long commented on the "irregularities" of Matthew's genealogy, especially its inclusion of women in the chain, an unusual occurrence in Jewish genealogy. St. Jerome saw Matthew choosing sinful women for his list, such as Rahab, but that is not so with Ruth. Others have suggested that he listed women who were foreigners, which is certainly true of Tamar, Rahab, and Ruth. Some have commented that this irregularity is the very thing these women have in common, thus preparing the ground for the "irregular" position of Mary, the virgin mother. Yet another motif is that each woman cited played an extraordinary personal role in the history of Israel.

In any case, it is clear that God worked in this people to prepare the coming of his Son, and he worked through a varied collection of persons. This should be a source of encouragement to us. God wanted to be with us through his Son; in achieving this, he worked through the lowly as well as the great. Should we not expect him to work among us today, in ways just as extraordinary, no matter what our status?

Whether we are high and mighty, or low and limited, God can use us to bring Jesus to others, just as Mary brought him to us. However irregular we may consider our position, the Father lets nothing stand in our way, not even ourselves. What joyful hope this should instill in us, that God would use us to bring his Son to others! Thus, in a sense, we can be part of the ongoing genealogy of Christ.

"Father, all generation begins with you, and I thank you for loving us to the point of sending your Son to be one of us. Just as you prepared the world for his coming, prepare my heart that I may worthily receive him, and use me to bring him to others."

Matthew 1:18-25

18   Now the birth of Jesus Christ took place in this way. When his mother Mary had been betrothed to Joseph, before they came together she was found to be with child of the Holy Spirit; 19 and her husband Joseph, being a just man and unwilling to put her to shame, resolved to send her away.
20   But as he considered this, behold, an angel of the Lord appeared to him in a dream, saying, "Joseph, son of David, do not fear to take Mary your wife, for that which is conceived in her is of the Holy Spirit; 21 she will bear a son, and you shall call his name Jesus, for he will save his people from their sins." 22 All this took place to fulfil what the Lord had spoken by the prophet: 23 "Behold, a virgin shall conceive and bear a son, and his name shall be called Emmanuel" (which means, God with us). 24 When Joseph woke from sleep, he did as the angel of the Lord commanded him; he took his wife, 25 but knew her not until she had borne a son; and he called his name Jesus.

Let the Lord enter; he is the King of Glory. (Psalm 24:7)

Joseph is one of the great examples in the Bible of what can happen when people cooperate with God. Even before the angel spoke to him, he had determined to protect Mary, at the risk of his own standing in the community. Simply on Mary's testimony that she was "with child of the Holy Spirit" (Matthew 1:18), Joseph trusted God and chose what he considered to be the safest path for the woman he had planned to make his wife. His trust was rewarded when the angel confirmed Mary's words and told him that the child to be born was destined to save his people from sin. (1:21)

Joseph believed in God's plan and worked to see it fulfilled; thus, the Messiah was born. The wonder and glory of all God's promises came to fruition, in part through the cooperation of this humble and upright man. In a unique way, he anticipated St. Paul's words that, through Christ, "we have received grace and apostleship to bring about the obedience of faith for the sake of his name" (Romans 1:5). Joseph clearly demonstrated the "obedience of faith", his simple trust in God showed that he was open to the grace God was pouring out to him.

In baptism, we too have received grace and apostleship. We have been called to the obedience of faith—not a slavish obedience of fear and anxiety, but an obedience based on love and simple trust. Like Paul and like Joseph, we are called to work with the Lord, to cooperate with him in his desire to bring all people into his kingdom. No matter how we may experience this call, we cannot remain passive. Rather, we are called to dedicate our whole being—body and soul—to the Lord's work. As we cooperate with him, we—like Joseph—will see marvelous things take place.

The birth of Christ marks the dawning of our redemption. Let us heed the voice of the psalmist and let the Lord, the King of

Glory, enter our hearts. Let us put aside sin and indifference and ask Christ, our King, to remove any obstacles that might hinder his coming in more fully. Let us take hold of the grace that is available to us.

Matthew 2:1-12

[1] Now when Jesus was born in Bethlehem of Judea in the days of Herod the king, behold, wise men from the East came to Jerusalem, saying, [2] "Where is he who has been born king of the Jews? For we have seen his star in the East, and have come to worship him." [3] When Herod the king heard this, he was troubled, and all Jerusalem with him; [4] and assembling all the chief priests and scribes of the people, he inquired of them where the Christ was to be born. [5] They told him, "In Bethlehem of Judea; for so it is written by the prophet: [6] 'And you, O Bethlehem, in the land of Judah, are by no means least among the rulers of Judah; for from you shall come a ruler who will govern my people Israel.' "

[7] Then Herod summoned the wise men secretly and ascertained from them what time the star appeared; [8] and he sent them to Bethlehem, saying, "Go and search diligently for the child, and when you have found him bring me word, that I too may come and worship him." [9] When they had heard the king they went their way; and lo, the star which they had seen in the East went before them, till it came to rest over the place where the child was. [10] When they saw the star, they rejoiced exceedingly with great joy; [11] and going into the house they saw the child with Mary his mother, and they fell down and worshiped him. Then, opening their treasures, they offered him gifts, gold and frankincense and myrrh. [12] And being

warned in a dream not to return to Herod, they departed to their own country by another way.

After the devastation of sin and the darkening of humanity; after centuries of preparation and longing, which included no less than the founding of an entire people set apart for God; after wars, division, exile, and foreign domination; after a lowly birth to a humble Jewish couple; after all this, the eternal Son of God was finally manifested to the nations. Herod took notice and feared for his kingdom. As the light of salvation dawned on the earth, the wise men of other nations recognized and paid homage to the one in whom all wisdom and dominion and power is found.

This revelation of Christ must have been powerful indeed! Sages from the East, men of learning, comfortable in their own kingdoms, were drawn to him. What could have induced them to leave their homes and positions of prominence behind to undertake such a long journey? Only a work of God in their hearts could have moved them to recognize the one they were coming to worship.

Fathers of the church have held that the sages' gifts reveal that they recognized—even if only to a small extent—who this baby was: Gold was tribute for a king; incense was offered as praise to God; and myrrh was ointment used to soothe the sufferings of humanity. Yet all three were presented to Jesus, for as true God and true man, he had been given all authority and dominion as King and Lord. By offering these three gifts, the wise men pointed to Jesus' authority, his deity, and the fact that the long-awaited salvation could only come about through his suffering and death.

What fruit was borne from the journey of these wise men! In their wake, generation after generation of the wise have bowed down before the humble child of Nazareth. Like the wealth of the nations in the prophet's words (Isaiah 60:5), men and women from every age have laid their treasures before Christ, renouncing the apparent wealth of this world to embrace the real wealth that is found in repentance, faith, and humility.

Let us imitate the faith and trust of the first wise men. In prayer, ask the Holy Spirit to reveal Christ to you. Ask the Spirit to help you pour out the wealth of your heart before Jesus and to accept his salvation and mercy. Our Light has come. Let us arise before him and greet him as he deserves.

Matthew 2:13-23

[13] Now when they had departed, behold, an angel of the Lord appeared to Joseph in a dream and said, "Rise, take the child and his mother, and flee to Egypt, and remain there till I tell you; for Herod is about to search for the child, to destroy him." [14] And he rose and took the child and his mother by night, and departed to Egypt, [15] and remained there until the death of Herod. This was to fulfil what the Lord had spoken by the prophet, "Out of Egypt have I called my son."

[16] Then Herod, when he saw that he had been tricked by the wise men, was in a furious rage, and he sent and killed all the male children in Bethlehem and in all that region who were two years old or under, according to the time which he had ascertained from the wise men. [17] Then was fulfilled what was spoken by the prophet Jeremiah: [18] "A voice was heard in Ramah, wailing and loud

lamentation, Rachel weeping for her children; she refused to be consoled, because they were no more." [19] But when Herod died, behold, an angel of the Lord appeared in a dream to Joseph in Egypt, saying, [20] "Rise, take the child and his mother, and go to the land of Israel, for those who sought the child's life are dead." [21] And he rose and took the child and his mother, and went to the land of Israel. [22] But when he heard that Archelaus reigned over Judea in place of his father Herod, he was afraid to go there, and being warned in a dream he withdrew to the district of Galilee. [23] And he went and dwelt in a city called Nazareth, that what was spoken by the prophets might be fulfilled, "He shall be called a Nazarene."

A s foster father and protector of the long-awaited Messiah, Joseph was God's representative, the shadow of God the Father, the one through whom Jesus would learn about his heavenly Father. In this role, Joseph can serve us today as a model parent and teach us much about family life.

First and foremost, Joseph was a godly man who heard from the Lord. The fact that an angel spoke to him (Matthew 1:20, 2:13) only serves to emphasize the importance of the message. That the message came from God himself is unquestionable: We can only believe that Joseph was open to God's word because he was a "just man" (1:19) who loved and was faithful to God.

Parents today, no less than in biblical times, need to hear from God. For us, this involves a special commitment to prayer and scripture reading. God wants us to know that the Holy Spirit who dwells in us can teach us how to nurture our families. The gifts of the Spirit (including wisdom and understanding, counsel and knowledge—see Isaiah 11:2, 1 Corinthians 12:7-11) can help parents shepherd their families along the way of the Lord.

Empowered by the wisdom of God, Joseph could see the forces of evil in the world (personified by Herod) and took steps to protect his son from them. We, too, need to protect our children from the real threats of the world. This does not mean running away or hiding our children from reality; it means teaching them and training them in the ways of God. If we can protect and teach our children—especially in the early, developmental years (and later in their lives as well)—they will grow in their ability to make decisions based on the truths of the gospel.

Joseph loved his son enough that he was willing to take the steps necessary to safeguard him, even though it was inconvenient to do so. When he learned of Herod's plot, he willingly uprooted himself and moved to Egypt—a largely pagan land in the eyes of a devout Jew. Can we trust the Lord enough to follow him, even when it is difficult and inconvenient? Let us seek the Lord's wisdom for our families. Like Joseph, we, too, must be the protectors and teachers of our children, leading them in the ways of salvation.

Matthew 3:1-12

[1] In those days came John the Baptist, preaching in the wilderness of Judea, [2] "Repent, for the kingdom of heaven is at hand." [3] For this is he who was spoken of by the prophet Isaiah when he said, "The voice of one crying in the wilderness: Prepare the way of the Lord, make his paths straight." [4] Now

John wore a garment of camel's hair, and a leather girdle around his waist; and his food was locusts and wild honey. [5] Then went out to him Jerusalem and all Judea and all the region about the Jordan, [6] and they were baptized by him in the river Jordan, confessing their sins.

[7] But when he saw many of the Pharisees and Sadducees coming for baptism, he said to them, "You brood of vipers! Who warned you to flee from the wrath to come? [8] Bear fruit that befits repentance, [9] and do not presume to say to yourselves, 'We have Abraham as our father'; for I tell you, God is able from these stones to raise up children to Abraham. [10] Even now the axe is laid to the root of the trees; every tree therefore that does not bear good fruit is cut down and thrown into the fire.

[11] "I baptize you with water for repentance, but he who is coming after me is mightier than I, whose sandals I am not worthy to carry; he will baptize you with the Holy Spirit and with fire. [12] His winnowing fork is in his hand, and he will clear his threshing floor and gather his wheat into the granary, but the chaff he will burn with unquenchable fire."

Preaching in the desert of Judea, John the Baptist had but one message for all who came to be baptized: "Repent, for the kingdom of heaven is at hand. . . . 'Prepare the way of the Lord, make his paths straight' "(Matthew 3:2,3). John understood that repentance and conversion, that radical interior turning away from sin and toward God, is essential for everyone who would come to share in the salvation of the Messiah. In these days, such a change of heart and subsequent change of behavior are still essential as we prepare for Jesus' coming among us again. We admit—perhaps too casually—that change is necessary in our lives, but what of our personal willingness to be changed in the ways God wants, not just in the ways we deem appropriate?

What of our desire to allow the Holy Spirit to convict us of sin patterns and mind sets that are a barrier to God's work in our lives? It is not just a matter of being a nicer or better person to our families, or keeping our heads in a difficult situation. We must get to the root of the pride and selfishness that cause us to treat others with little or no respect, to be unconcerned about their needs. It is necessary to strike at the root of the resentments and unforgiveness that are causing division in our families, our communities, our parish relationships.

In baptism, we received the Spirit of Jesus, a Spirit of power and new life. All activity of the Spirit is directed toward helping us draw close to God and so share more fully in his divine life. Therefore, the Spirit's purpose in convicting us of sin is to give us life by revealing to us where our sin brings death. It is to aid us in believing that God truly wants to make us what he intended when he first created us in his own image and likeness. The Spirit helps us to recognize the discrepancies between the life we now lead and the one he wants us to lead as privileged sharers in God's divine life.

Let us pray to recognize, renounce, and repent of our sinfulness. As we bring forth the fruit of love, forgiveness, and reconciliation, we will be better able to appropriate our heritage as sons and daughters of God, in Christ. We, too, will prepare for Jesus' coming, making ready the way of the Lord and making his path straight.

Matthew 3:13-17

[13] Then Jesus came from Galilee to the Jordan to John, to be baptized by him. [14] John would have prevented him, saying, "I need to be baptized by you, and do you come to me?" [15] But Jesus answered him, "Let it be so now; for thus it is fitting for us to fulfil all righteousness." Then he consented. [16] And when Jesus was baptized, he went up immediately from the water, and behold, the heavens were opened and he saw the Spirit of God descending like a dove, and alighting on him; [17] and lo, a voice from heaven, saying, "This is my beloved Son, with whom I am well pleased."

After years of waiting and preparing, the time had come for Jesus to take up his mission. No longer would he remain hidden away in Nazareth, quietly plying his trade as a carpenter. Now was the time to play his part in the Father's plan, the time to announce and to inaugurate the kingdom of God. Now was the time for healings, exorcisms, preaching, and teaching.

This great kingdom was not to begin with a blare of trumpets or a mighty demonstration of miracles. It would begin not in glory, but in humility, as Jesus submitted himself to baptism of repentance. He, the sinless one, would heed the Baptizer's call to sinners. The one who had been clothed in glory would bow to one clothed in rough garments. He, the righteous one, would identify himself with sinners to fulfill all righteousness.

Matthew said that when Jesus came up out of the water, the

Spirit descended on him and the Father testified to him, declaring him to be his "beloved Son," and that he was "well pleased" with him (Matthew 3:16-17). By recounting Jesus' baptism in this way, Matthew emphasized Jesus' role as the servant of the Lord who was identified in Isaiah 42:1-7. Like the servant in Isaiah, Jesus had come to "bring forth justice," to open blind eyes, and to release prisoners (Isaiah 42:3,7). Even more importantly, like the servant of the Lord, he had come to make a sin offering of himself, bearing others' sins and interceding for their forgiveness (53:10,12).

St Paul said that at our baptism we were baptized into Christ (Romans 6:3, Galatians 3:27). Jesus' baptism was *our* baptism as well. Just as the Spirit descended on Jesus, so too the Spirit comes upon us when we are baptized. Just as the Father declared Jesus to be his beloved Son, we too become beloved sons and daughters of God at our baptism. Just as Jesus took up his commission as a servant, we too are called to lay down our lives for the upbuilding of the kingdom.

Confident in the Spirit's anointing and filled with the humility of Christ, let us take up our high calling to serve our Father with the joy and abandonment of dearly loved sons and daughters.

Matthew 4:1-11

[1] Then Jesus was led up by the Spirit into the wilderness to be tempted by the devil. [2] And he fasted forty days and forty nights, and afterward he was hungry. [3] And the tempter came and said to him, "If you are the Son of God, command these stones to become loaves of bread." [4] But he answered, "It is written, 'Man

shall not live by bread alone, but by every word that proceeds from the mouth of God.' "

5   Then the devil took him to the holy city, and set him on the pinnacle of the temple, [6] and said to him, "If you are the Son of God, throw yourself down; for it is written, 'He will give his angels charge of you,' and 'On their hands they will bear you up, lest you strike your foot against a stone.' " [7] Jesus said to him, "Again it is written, 'You shall not tempt the Lord your God.' "

8   Again, the devil took him to a very high mountain, and showed him all the kingdoms of the world and the glory of them; [9] and he said to him, "All these I will give you, if you will fall down and worship me." [10] Then Jesus said to him, "Begone, Satan! for it is written, 'You shall worship the Lord your God and him only shall you serve.' " [11] Then the devil left him, and behold, angels came and ministered to him.

To most people, reality is that which we can see, touch, hear, smell, and taste; it is the world around us. For the Christian, however, reality extends beyond the physical environment and encompasses a whole spiritual realm as well, both the glory of heaven and Satan's realm of darkness. The devil is a reality of our world, and he is opposed to us, waging war against us day and night.

Satan's temptation of Jesus reveals three of the key ways in which he works. First, he may try to persuade us to use spiritual power or authority to benefit ourselves. For instance, people serving in the church may be tempted to use their positions of trust to get people to serve them. Parents (or others in authority) may be tempted to do the same regarding those in their care. Second, Satan often tries to persuade us to bargain with God, perhaps enticing us to try to convince God to act in a certain way in exchange for our prayers or service without regard for his will. Finally, he tries to deceive us into worshipping idols instead of God, things like money, fame, possessions, or status.

The Prince of Darkness wants us to follow his thinking in times of temptation, turning away from God. We face this choice every day: Will we succumb to Satan and his seemingly logical arguments or will we renounce him and choose obedience to the Father? Yielding to Satan, even in small matters, is always dangerous. He is completely opposed to God; he wants nothing more than the destruction of Christ's church and all who follow him.

We are not alone in our efforts to resist the devil. Paul wrote the Romans: "The free gift in the grace of that one man Jesus Christ abounded for many" (Romans 5:15). The letter to the Hebrews says: "Because he himself has suffered and been tempted, he [Jesus] is able to help those who are tempted" (Hebrews 2:18). Because Jesus was tempted as we are and triumphed, we can share in his victory. Because he destroyed the work of the devil (1 John 3:8) by his death to sin and resurrection to new life, Jesus has won protection and deliverance for all who die and rise with him in faith. We can look to Jesus in time of temptation and receive from him an abundance of grace and strength to resist the devil.

Matthew 4:12-25

[12]   Now when he heard that John had been arrested, he withdrew into Galilee; [13] and leaving Nazareth he went and dwelt in Capernaum by the sea, in the territory of Zebulun and Naphtali, [14] that what was spoken by the prophet Isaiah might be fulfilled: [15] "The land of Zebulun and the land of Naphtali, toward the sea, across the Jordan, Galilee of the Gentiles—[16] the people who sat in darkness have seen a great light, and for those who sat in the region and shadow of death light has dawned." [17] From that time Jesus began to preach, saying, "Repent, for the kingdom of heaven is at hand."

[18]   As he walked by the Sea of Galilee, he saw two brothers, Simon who is called Peter and Andrew his brother, casting a net into the sea; for they were fishermen. [19] And he said to them, "Follow me, and I will make you fishers of men." [20] Immediately they left their nets and followed him. [21] And going on from there he saw two other brothers, James the son of Zebedee and John his brother, in the boat with Zebedee their father, mending their nets, and he called them. [22] Immediately they left the boat and their father, and followed him.

[23]   And he went about all Galilee, teaching in their synagogues and preaching the gospel of the kingdom and healing every disease and every infirmity among the people. [24] So his fame spread throughout all Syria, and they brought him all the sick, those afflicted with various diseases and pains, demoniacs, epileptics, and paralytics, and he healed them. [25] And great crowds followed him from Galilee and the Decapolis and Jerusalem and Judea and from beyond the Jordan.

Following the arrest of John the Baptist, Jesus returned to Galilee to begin his public ministry. He called the disciples who would share that ministry with him by becoming "fishers of men"—first among the chosen people and then beyond the Jews to the Gentiles. Like Jesus, their work would be "teaching in their synagogues and preaching the gospel of the kingdom and healing every disease and every infirmity among the people" (Matthew 4:23).

The three-fold mission of Jesus—preaching, teaching, healing—which began in Galilee is now the responsibility of the church:

> For the Lord Jesus inaugurated her (the church) by preaching the Good News, that is the coming of God's kingdom: "The time is fulfilled and the kingdom of God is at hand." This kingdom shone out before men in the words, in the works and the presence of Christ. (Vatican II, *Constitution on the Church*, 5)

Just as the preaching and teaching of Jesus was accompanied by healings and miracles, so will we be faithful to our mission by eagerly pursuing each of these elements in the world today. To the extent that these signs are visible and life-giving, are we able to reveal Jesus as the Son of God and extend his kingdom on earth.

As members of the body of Christ, we have all been called to participate in the church's mission in these ways. Throughout our lives, we will be given many opportunities to proclaim the gospel, teach others about Jesus, and pray expectantly for physical, emotional, or spiritual healing. Let us be careful not to allow fear, complacency, or doubts about God's power to block us from becoming vessels of the grace of Christ.

Let us pray that "the church, the kingdom of Christ, now present in mystery, grows visibly in the world through the power of

God" in the exercise of her three-fold mission (*Constitution on the Church*, 3). Let us beg God to remove from our hearts any barriers to desiring the full work of the church, which is the work of Christ, to take place.

The Sermon on the Mount

MATTHEW
5–7

Matthew 5:1-12

[1] Seeing the crowds, he went up on the mountain, and when he sat down his disciples came to him. [2] And he opened his mouth and taught them, saying: [3] "Blessed are the poor in spirit, for theirs is the kingdom of heaven. [4] "Blessed are those who mourn, for they shall be comforted. [5] "Blessed are the meek, for they shall inherit the earth. [6] "Blessed are those who hunger and thirst for righteousness, for they shall be satisfied. [7] "Blessed are the merciful, for they shall obtain mercy. [8] "Blessed are the pure in heart, for they shall see God. [9] "Blessed are the peacemakers, for they shall be called sons of God. [10] "Blessed are those who are persecuted for righteousness' sake, for theirs is the kingdom of heaven.

[11] "Blessed are you when men revile you and persecute you and utter all kinds of evil against you falsely on my account. [12] Rejoice and be glad, for your reward is great in heaven, for so men persecuted the prophets who were before you."

The Greek word for "blessed"—*makarios*—carries two kinds of meanings in scripture. The "blessed" one is described as the recipient of divine favor, and also as one who is "happy" or "fortunate." In the beatitudes, Jesus combined these meanings, giving us a road map to help us find not only happiness, but the blessing and grace of God in our lives.

How jarring these beatitudes must have seemed to the people who first heard Jesus speak them—just as they jar us today! How can the poor and the meek, the merciful and pure in heart, even the persecuted, consider themselves happy? Wouldn't you naturally recoil from such a description? This is precisely why Jesus' words can be so challenging: Reality is not always what we see immediately in front of us.

Jesus had nowhere to lay his head (Matthew 8:20) and was often misunderstood and treated with suspicion. Yet he was the most peaceful and joyful man to ever walk the earth. Why? Because he treasured his Father's presence and his commands above all else. Jesus had learned that those who entrust themselves to God will never be disappointed, and he invited his disciples to experience this blessing for themselves. He invites us all to become like him: poor in spirit, meek, merciful, hungering after righteousness, and pure in heart. And, ever true to his promises, he has given us his Holy Spirit to teach us and empower us to follow this path. His life within us is will always bring us true happiness.

When he described the rewards of such a life, Jesus used the future tense, because he wanted to extend our vision beyond our earthly life to the kingdom he had come to inaugurate. We *will* be comforted, we *will* be satisfied, we *will* obtain mercy, and we *will* see God (Matthew 5:4-8). By faithfully answering God's invitation to participate in his divine nature on earth, we are sure to receive untold blessings in the life to come.

The beatitudes require a reorientation in us. The life God offers us may seem too costly at first. We may think we are too weak to accept it. We may not want to embrace a life that seems so demanding. With eyes of faith, however, we can trust in Jesus' promises. Our life in Christ will bring blessings to ourselves as well as others here on earth, and even greater blessings in heaven.

Matthew 5:13-16

13 "You are the salt of the earth; but if salt has lost its taste, how shall its saltness be restored? It is no longer good for anything except to be thrown out and trodden under foot by men.
14 "You are the light of the world. A city set on a hill cannot be hid. 15 Nor do men light a lamp and put it under a bushel, but on a stand, and it gives light to all in the house. 16 Let your light so shine before men, that they may see your good works and give glory to your Father who is in heaven."

Considering the condition and status of followers, Jesus' pronouncement was truly startling. While there might have been a few notables or scholars in attendance, the people who had gathered on the mountainside were mostly the poor, the sick, the uneducated, the unimportant of society. Yet, Jesus told them: "You are the salt of the earth . . . you are the light of the world" (Matthew 5:13,14).

Jesus was defining the role of discipleship. Just as salt makes food more tasty while also preserving it, so were his followers to witness to the truth as well as sustain it. Like the small lamps of those days which provided the only light in homes, the disciples would be the only light in a darkened world. How could they do this? By being a reflection of the one who said: "I am the light of the world" (John 8:12).

How often do we hear people say: "Religion is a private affair. My faith is a matter between God and me." That is the opposite of what Jesus told his disciples. He counseled against restricting the light to private use and urged instead that it be allowed to beam out to others. Why? To win acclaim, rewards, or acceptance? No, it was to give glory to the Father in heaven (Matthew 5:16). All that Jesus did gave glory to his Father, and he exhorted his disciples to work for the glory of his and *their* Father.

Jesus was not telling his disciples that by doing good works, they would earn salvation. Rather, he was saying that the works they did would be a proclamation of the faith in their hearts. Just as it is the very nature of salt to flavor and preserve, so it is the very nature of light to shine and illuminate what is around it. Similarly, it must be the nature of Jesus' disciples to reflect his light to a darkened world so that all people will see, know, and glorify the Father in heaven.

"Father, we are but poor reflections of your beloved Son, Jesus. Help us today to focus and intensify the light in us so that it will illuminate everyone we meet. Spirit of light, burn brightly in us to the glory of the Father through Jesus Christ, his Son."

Matthew 5:17-19

[17] "Think not that I have come to abolish the law and the prophets; I have come not to abolish them but to fulfill them. [18] For truly, I say to you, till heaven and earth pass away, not an iota, not a dot, will pass from the law until all is accomplished. [19] Whoever then relaxes one of the least of these commandments and teaches men so, shall be called least in the kingdom of heaven; but he who does them and teaches them shall be called great in the kingdom of heaven."

In the Old Testament, God revealed himself and gave direction to his people through the law and the prophets. The law began with the ten commandments that were given to Moses on Mount Sinai (Exodus 20). God's prophets were men and women whom he called to speak his word to the people. In Hebrew scripture, the material referred to as "the prophets" is made up of the books of Joshua, Judges, Samuel, Kings, Isaiah, Jeremiah, Ezekiel, and the twelve minor prophets.

As the Word of God who came into the world, Jesus is the fulfillment of all the things God had spoken about through the law and prophets. The word "fulfill" means to make complete, or to supply what is lacking. In this text, the meaning of "fulfill" is expanded to include the perfecting of something that is imperfect. Jesus recognized that the laws of Moses and the prophets were good but imperfect. Thus, he came "not to abolish them but to fulfill them" and said that anyone who relaxed even "the least of these commandments . . . shall be called least in the kingdom of heaven" (Matthew 5:17,19).

Matthew's gospel goes on to identify six areas in which the law was to be perfected and fulfilled: Murder, adultery, divorce, oaths, revenge, and love of enemies (5:21-48). Through his death and resurrection, Jesus has made it possible for us to live as it was first set out in the law and the prophets. Jesus even said that not one "iota" or "dot" of the law was to be set aside (Matthew 5:18). "Iota" is the smallest letter of the Hebrew alphabet, and the "dot" designates a small decorative marking which is added to many Hebrew consonants in the square script. Jesus' point was that the way of life set forth by the law and the prophets was good and, in him, we could live it out.

How can our righteousness exceed that of the scribes and the Pharisees? We have what they did not have: We have Jesus dwelling in us through the power of the Spirit. By our own merits, we are unable to keep the commandments; with Jesus in us, we have the strength and understanding to obey. Jesus has perfectly kept the law and fulfilled God's word that came to us through the prophets. By faith and baptism into his death and resurrection, we are given the power to live a whole new life of obedience to the Father.

Let us imitate the faith and trust of the first wise men. In prayer, ask the Holy Spirit to reveal Christ to you and to empower you to keep his commands. Pray especially for the grace to surrender your life to the Father so that he can fill you with his life and power.

Matthew 5:20-26

[20] "For I tell you, unless your righteousness exceeds that of the scribes and Pharisees, you will never enter the kingdom of heaven. [21] "You have heard that it was said to the men of old, 'You shall not kill; and whoever kills shall be liable to judgment.' [22] But I say to you that every one who is angry with his brother shall be liable to judgment; whoever insults his brother shall be liable to the council, and whoever says, 'You fool!' shall be liable to the hell of fire. [23] So if you are offering your gift at the altar, and there remember that your brother has something against you, [24] leave your gift there before the altar and go; first be reconciled to your brother, and then come and offer your gift. [25] Make friends quickly with your accuser, while you are going with him to court, lest your accuser hand you over to the judge, and the judge to the guard, and you be put in prison; [26] truly, I say to you, you will never get out till you have paid the last penny."

Hardly a day goes by that we don't learn from the news media of another murder. We are appalled at these acts and feel quite self-righteous before God in comparison to those committing the murder. This is the kind of righteousness that characterized the Pharisees and the scribes. Jesus said that unless our righteousness exceeded that of the scribes and Pharisees we would never enter the kingdom of heaven (Matthew 5:20). He was telling us that being right with the Lord does not depend solely on refraining from acts prohibited by the law, but on the condition of our hearts in our relationships with our neighbors and with God.

Instead of feeling self-satisfied because we are not murderers, let us examine our hearts to see the angers or resentments we may have toward others. Our resentments and hatreds, even though we hold them in check, violate the greatest commandment Jesus taught us: Love of God and love of neighbor (Matthew 22:37-40). Our proper response is clear: We need to repent and be reconciled (5:24). It is not enough to say, "I should not be angry with my spouse or children or teacher. I should not be jealous of that co-worker. I should not resent my boss for correcting me or for not appreciating the things I do." The kingdom of heaven calls for reconciliation, not just an acknowledgment of wrongful thoughts or acts.

In a talk given in the Netherlands in 1985, Pope John Paul II put it this way: "External observance of the law has no great value if the heart is blind or wicked . . . . The heart, in other words the conscience, must be purified and informed . . . . Christ reveals to his disciples that here is a value that surpasses all others and binds them together: Love. This law of love, which contains the Law and the Prophets, must become the law of their conscience."

Let us pray today: "Heavenly Father, through the work of the Holy Spirit, give me the ability to see the angers and resentments I hold toward others. Help me to look across the years to recall the people I have not forgiven, especially my relatives. I ask for the desire and courage to seek reconciliation. Melt my pride and help me to delay no longer. I pray this in the name of Jesus."

Matthew 5:27-32

27 "You have heard that it was said, 'You shall not commit adultery.' 28 But I say to you that every one who looks at a woman lustfully has already committed adultery with her in his heart. 29 If your right eye causes you to sin, pluck it out and throw it away; it is better that you lose one of your members than that your whole body be thrown into hell.

30 And if your right hand causes you to sin, cut it off and throw it away; it is better that you lose one of your members than that your whole body go into hell.

31 "It was also said, 'Whoever divorces his wife, let him give her a certificate of divorce.' 32 But I say to you that every one who divorces his wife, except on the ground of unchastity, makes her an adulteress; and whoever marries a divorced woman commits adultery."

Matthew's Gospel was carefully arranged to portray Jesus as the Messiah who inaugurated the long-awaited kingdom of God. In the discourse called the Sermon on the Mount, Matthew presented Jesus' invitation to those who would enter this kingdom. He first described its unique blessings—the Beatitudes. Then, like a new Moses, Jesus introduced a series of intrinsic principles of the messianic reign.

In light of the coming of the kingdom, Jesus taught his followers how to live so that the life of God would take root and grow in their lives. He spoke about many of the challenges we face in our daily lives: The call to righteousness, turning away from anger, swearing, and revenge, and the need to love our enemies. The precepts followed a set pattern: "You have heard that it was said, . . . but I say to you . . . ." This new ethic surpassed the laws of Moses and the Pharisees. Jesus, as the promised Messiah, fulfilled "the law and the prophets" (Matthew 5:17).

Jesus' vision transcended the letter of the law: The Old Testament command, "You shall not commit adultery," became, "Every one who looks at a woman lustfully has already committed adultery with her in his heart" (Matthew 5:28). Jesus shifted focus to the heart, penetrating the legalities to expose Moses' deeper intention. Using a typical rabbinical style of discourse, Jesus suggested that believers might even be better off sacrificing eyes or limbs—if that were necessary—to gain the kingdom (Matthew 5:29-30). This emphasized the need to root out our innermost drives to sin.

Matthew's account of Jesus' position on divorce shattered the natural preconceptions held by those who heard him (witness the disciples' protestations in Matthew 19:10). The words here were not intended to condemn persons to remain forever in destructive relationships, but to point to the grace God gives to married couples to live in a way that advances the kingdom of God. Like the Beatitudes and the call to love our enemies, they reveal the radically different way of life inaugurated by Jesus.

To live up to this new way requires an inner work of the Spirit. Through faith, we can experience the power to love others as Christ loved us. Let us ask the Lord to give this grace to all of us: "Jesus, please empower us through your grace to love each other and to be pure in heart. We confess that we cannot truly love unless you transform us from within. Send your Spirit so that we may embrace your wonderful invitation to enter your kingdom."

Matthew 5:33-37

³³ "Again you have heard that it was said to the men of old, 'You shall not swear falsely, but shall perform to the Lord what you have sworn.' ³⁴ But I say to you, Do not swear at all, either by heaven, for it is the throne of God, ³⁵ or by the earth, for it is his footstool, or by Jerusalem, for it is the city of the great King. ³⁶ And do not swear by your head, for you cannot make one hair white or black. ³⁷ Let what you say be simply 'Yes' or 'No'; anything more than this comes from evil."

The Old Testament clearly allowed oath-taking: "You shall not swear by my name falsely, and so profane the name of your God" (Leviticus 19:12). However, in Jesus' time, oath-taking sometimes led to untruthfulness because loopholes were created to allow oath-takers to escape their commitment.

How startling Jesus' words must have sounded to his listeners! He called his followers to a higher standard of truthfulness, one in which a person's word could be depended on, without the necessity of an oath. Our trustworthiness should be so great that it would be unnecessary to invoke God's name and all that he rules—heaven and earth, Jerusalem, or even our own "heads" (Matthew 5:36).

Trust and integrity are the foundation stones of our relationships. Relationships grow strong and deep when there is mutual trust. Other people, especially those close to us, need to be able to depend on us and believe that what we say is what we mean and what we will do. Without trust, love can be stifled.

If we begin to feel comfortable with our dishonesty, we can easily deceive ourselves as well as others. We may never see the patterns of sin in our lives that are blocking God's love and our growth in holiness. We can never deceive God, however, who is able to look into our hearts and know what lies there. Honesty is the lifeblood of our relationship with God.

Our honesty and consistent faithfulness to gospel standards can be a powerful witness to a world that is skeptical and ready to find hypocrisy among those who profess to be Christians. When we call ourselves followers of Christ, we say, in effect, that we will follow the standards that Christ established. We can bear witness to the gospel with more than words; our lifestyles and our actions reveal to the world the true depth of our faith.

"Lord Jesus, I want to be your witness to an unbelieving world. Please cleanse me of the sin that causes my inconsistencies. Wash me with your blood so that I may be more faithful to you and a more credible witness to others. Send your Holy Spirit to give me the strength and desire to live out my Christian calling."

Matthew 5:38-42

[38] "You have heard that it was said, 'An eye for an eye and a tooth for a tooth.' [39] But I say to you, Do not resist one who is evil. But if any one strikes you on the right cheek, turn to him the other also; [40] and if any one would sue you and take your coat, let him have your cloak as well; [41] and if any one forces you to go one mile, go with him two miles. [42] Give to him who begs from you, and do not refuse him who would borrow from you."

At first glance, the Old Testament teaching about revenge (an eye for an eye and a tooth for a tooth—see Exodus 21:24) might seem somewhat vindictive. In fact, however, God gave this law to prevent people from inflicting undue or inordinate punishment upon one another. The law prevents retribution from being greater than the offense that evoked it. This teaching about revenge is the fifth example Matthew used to illustrate Jesus' statement that he came to fulfill the law and the prophets, not abolish them (Matthew 5:17). Only in Jesus can the wall of hostility between people be broken down.

The new teaching on forgiveness rather than revenge was—and still is—difficult to accept. It runs counter to all that we, as fallen men and women, have in our hearts concerning how to relate to others. If we are wronged, for instance, we feel we have the right to retaliate. When we are hurt, whether verbally or physically, we feel justified in seeking revenge. Our focus on our *rights* and on *justice* causes us to separate ourselves from our brothers and sisters and raise ourselves above them.

Jesus died on the cross so that all people could be united in one body—*his* body. He wants his people to live in unity. In order for this to occur, however, we need to obey God's command to love him and to love one another. This command, which was most perfectly lived out by Jesus, is the first obligation we have as sons and daughters of God (Matthew 22:37-39).

Jesus gives us the power every day to live out his command to love and forgive one another. When we are wronged, our first response must be to say in our hearts that we believe Jesus died on the cross for everyone; that his victory is stronger than our hunger for revenge. We can then ask God for the grace to forgive, to return good for evil. The more we live this out, the stronger will the love of God grow within us.

"Lord Jesus, I believe that through your cross you drew all people to yourself. Help me to forgive, rather than condemn; to love, rather than criticize; to care beyond what I think is expected of me. In this way, I will grow in my love for you and for my neighbor."

Matthew 5:43-48

[43] "You have heard that it was said, 'You shall love your neighbor and hate your enemy.' [44] But I say to you, Love your enemies and pray for those who persecute you, [45] so that you may be sons of your Father who is in heaven; for he makes his sun rise on the evil and on the good, and sends rain on the just and on the unjust. [46] For if you love those who love you, what reward have you? Do not even the tax collectors do the same? [47] And if you salute only your brethren, what more are you doing than others? Do not even the Gentiles do the same? [48] You, therefore, must be perfect, as your heavenly Father is perfect."

The eternal Father looked down from heaven and his heart was touched with compassion. He saw the misery that had overtaken the people he had created, but who had turned from him in sin. In love, he sent his Son, Jesus, to live and die for us that we might be restored to him. How it must have brought joy to the Father to give the Holy Spirit, the love of God poured out, to those who were joined to Jesus through faith and baptism.

The love that is poured out to those who believe, is God's love—divine, infinite, eternal, deep. This is why we can go beyond our limited ways of loving when we believe in Jesus. By the power of the Holy Spirit, we can love not only those who love us, but our enemies as well—those who persecute us.

Jesus taught: "Be perfect . . . as your heavenly Father is perfect" (Matthew 5:48). This perfection has to do with our ability to be like Jesus and to love as he loved. This unselfish love of God always desires the best for our brothers and sisters. This love transforms us from within. The degree to which we have experienced God's love is the degree to which we can love others.

We can only learn to love as God loves when we "lean on the arm of the beloved." We can only love like Jesus when we are supported and upheld by the power of his abundant love dwelling in us. In our weakness, he becomes our strength.

In practical ways, how are we to love? Do we see how we have hurt our spouses, our children, our parents through our unloving ways? How do we love those in authority over us? Do we hold grudges and resentments? Do we make cutting or cynical remarks? Do we love those who are our neighbors—in our churches, communities, and in the neighborhood of the world? How about the poor and helpless, those who cannot defend themselves? Do we love those of different religions, racial groups, nationalities, and social classes?

Let us turn to Jesus and ask him to teach us how to love. As we see how we have failed to love, let us ask God's forgiveness and learn to lean on the arm of the beloved and love as Jesus has loved us.

Matthew 6:1-6, 16-18

1 "Beware of practicing your piety before men in order to be seen by them; for then you will have no reward from your Father who is in heaven.

2 "Thus, when you give alms, sound no trumpet before you, as the hypocrites do in the synagogues and in the streets, that they may be praised by men. Truly, I say to you, they have received their reward. 3 But when you give alms, do not let your left hand know what your right hand is doing, 4 so that your alms may be in secret; and your Father who sees in secret will reward you.

5 "And when you pray, you must not be like the hypocrites; for they love to stand and pray in the synagogues and at the street corners, that they may be seen by men. Truly, I say to you, they have received their reward. 6 But when you pray, go into your room and shut the door and pray to your Father who is in secret; and your Father who sees in secret will reward you.

16 "And when you fast, do not look dismal, like the hypocrites, for they disfigure their faces that their fasting may be seen by men. Truly, I say to you, they have received their reward. 17 But when you fast, anoint your head and wash your face, 18 that your fasting may not be seen by men but by your Father who is in secret; and your Father who sees in secret will reward you."

The practices of prayer, almsgiving, and fasting are grounded in Jewish tradition. In order for them to be credited to us as righteousness, they must be motivated by the love of God.

The New Law is called a *law of love* because it makes us act out of the love infused by the Holy Spirit, . . . *a law of grace*, because it confers the strength of grace to act, by means of faith and sacraments; *a law of freedom*, because it sets us free from the ritual and juridical observances of the Old Law. (*Catechism of the Catholic Church*, 1972)

Jesus admonished his followers: "When you fast, do not look dismal, like the hypocrites, for they disfigure their faces that their fasting may be seen by men" (Matthew 6:16). The word "hypocrite" in Greek means "actor," one who performs in front of others, pretending to be something he or she is not. A spiritual hypocrite is one whose motivation for pious conduct is self-glorification.

Almsgiving has to do with helping people—lending a hand, giving money, time, or resources to others. Fasting means abstaining from food or particular foods for certain periods of time, usually for spiritual reasons. Practices of this kind can—if they are humanly motivated—tend to draw attention to ourselves; if performed well, they can inflate our egos. If we fail to do these things well, they can lead to discouragement and despair.

Following these practices out of love for God and his people, however, can bring great joy and healing to our lives. Our works of charity are fruitful to the degree that they enable us to become less preoccupied with self. Jesus was always one with the Father, did the Father's will, and acted for the Father's honor and glory. He never sought to be noticed, to win public esteem or self glory. We too, through a living, personal relationship with Jesus and the infinite resources of divine grace, can practice true piety.

Mother Teresa said: "We must be aware of oneness with Christ, as he was aware of oneness with his Father. Our activity is truly apostolic only insofar as we permit him to work in us and through us with his power, with his desire, and with his love" (*Gift from God*, 74).

Matthew 6:7-15

[7] "And in praying do not heap up empty phrases as the Gentiles do; for they think that they will be heard for their many words. [8] Do not be like them, for your Father knows what you need before you ask him. [9] Pray then like this: Our Father who art in heaven, Hallowed be thy name. [10] Thy kingdom come. Thy will be done, On earth as it is in heaven. [11] Give us this day our daily bread; [12] And forgive us our debts, As we also have forgiven our debtors; [13] And lead us not into temptation, But deliver us from evil. [14] For if you forgive men their trespasses, your heavenly Father also will forgive you; [15] but if you do not forgive men their trespasses, neither will your Father forgive your trespasses."

Consider the prevailing attitudes of Jesus' contemporaries toward their God: They knew him as the all-powerful Creator, as the all-knowing one who had delivered them from slavery, as the all-caring God who had given them a homeland and provided for their needs. They also feared him and trembled at his name. So sacred was his name that they dared not even pronounce it, using other words instead to designate God.

Then came Jesus. When his disciples asked him to teach them how to pray, he began by telling them to address God as "Abba," roughly equivalent to "Dad." Jesus was not simply giving his disciples a new title for Yahweh. Prayer does not consist of a set of words, but is rather a disposition of the heart. He was revealing to his disciples that, as a result of his incarnation and his forthcoming death and resurrection, they would be able to relate to God in a totally new way—as his loving and beloved children.

The whole of the Lord's Prayer is predicated on this intimate relationship with God. We do not merely *call* him "Father;" he *is* our Father because we have become his adopted children through Jesus' blood. Because the Holy Spirit now dwells in us (the very same Spirit who dwells in Jesus), we are brought to true spiritual life in God. We share in the very holiness of Jesus, and thus we can say with him, "Abba."

It is only when our hearts know God in this way that we can bless his name and long for the coming of his kingdom. Only with hearts of loving children can we ask that his will be done here on earth. When we know God as Father, we can ask confidently for him to provide for our daily needs. As trusting children, we can beg our Father to ward off temptation and protect us from the evil one.

As we come to know Almighty God as Abba, the prayer Jesus taught his disciples will become the model for our whole prayer life and the foundation of our daily peace and joy. The beautiful words of the Our Father will penetrate our hearts and fill us with the glory of God.

Matthew 6:19-23

[19] "Do not lay up for yourselves treasures on earth, where moth and rust consume and where thieves break in and steal, [20] but lay up for yourselves treasures in heaven, where neither moth nor rust consumes and where thieves do not break in and steal. [21] For where your treasure is, there will your heart be also.

[22] "The eye is the lamp of the body. So, if your eye is sound, your whole body will be full of light; [23] but if your eye is not sound, your whole body will be full of darkness. If then the light in you is darkness, how great is the darkness!"

W hy do we so often think that a new car, a new home, or a luxury vacation will make us happy? Often it turns out that new possessions just complicate our already hectic lives. Material things may make us happy for awhile, but once their "newness" wears off, we can feel just as unfulfilled as before. In a consumer society, boredom with life acts as a signal to people that they "need" to buy something else.

Jesus knew that material things lose their luster; they can never fulfill the deepest longings of the human heart. Yet we cling desperately to what we can see, hear, and touch. We think that if our sensory appetites are satisfied, we will be also. But God has given us more than senses. He has given us a heart that wants to be loved and wants to love in return. He is the only thing that ultimately fulfills us.

St. Athanasius (c. 296-373) wrote in his account of the life of St. Antony of Egypt (c. 251-356) that Antony was challenged by

Jesus' words on wealth: He felt that "the words of the Gospel had been directed to him. He hurried out and made a gift of his inheritance . . . to the villagers for he did not want himself and his sister to be held back by property. He sold the rest of his goods and gave the money to the poor, except for a small sum which he reserved for his sister" (*Life of St. Antony*).

Antony took the words of the gospel literally. He realized that material things are often an obstacle in our walk with the Lord, obscuring our spiritual vision of God. While most of us have responsibilities that would prevent us from giving up everything as Antony did, we can still become "poor in spirit" (Matthew 5:3). By dedicating our lives to the Lord and his call for us, rather than focusing on earthly treasures, we will become more generous with our time and our money. With spiritual eyes, we will see the uselessness of acquiring "things," and the enduring value of serving the Lord and those he has put in our lives.

"Father in heaven, we want to be like your Son, Jesus. Help us to become poor in spirit, as he was, relying only on your providence. Help us to discern our 'wants' from our 'needs.' "

Matthew 6:24-34

24 "No one can serve two masters; for either he will hate the one and love the other, or he will be devoted to the one and despise the other. You cannot serve God and mammon.

25 "Therefore I tell you, do not be anxious about your life, what you shall eat or what you shall drink, nor about your body, what you shall put on. Is not life more than food, and the body more than clothing? 26 Look at the birds of the air: they neither sow nor reap nor gather into barns, and yet your heavenly Father feeds them. Are you not of more value than they? 27 And which of you by being anxious can add one cubit to his span of life? 28 And why are you anxious about clothing? Consider the lilies of the field, how they grow; they neither toil nor spin; 29 yet I tell you, even Solomon in all his glory was not arrayed like one of these. 30 But if God so clothes the grass of the field, which today is alive and tomorrow is thrown into the oven, will he not much more clothe you, O men of little faith? 31 Therefore do not be anxious, saying, 'What shall we eat?' or 'What shall we drink?' or 'What shall we wear?' 32 For the Gentiles seek all these things; and your heavenly Father knows that you need them all. 33 But seek first his kingdom and his righteousness, and all these things shall be yours as well.

34 "Therefore do not be anxious about tomorrow, for tomorrow will be anxious for itself. Let the day's own trouble be sufficient for the day."

When we consider the circumstances of those who heard Jesus' words, it may strike us as strange and unrealistic to tell them not to worry about tomorrow. After all, they were poor, oppressed people. They might have had good reason to be anxious about food and clothing. Nevertheless, Jesus challenged them to "seek first his kingdom and his righteousness, and all these things will be yours as well" (Matthew 6:33). Some of them may have dismissed his words as impractical optimism.

Yet Jesus spoke lovingly and sincerely, backing up his challenge to trust God with logic: If God clothed the fields and fed the birds (Matthew 6:26-30), would he not care for his children whom he loved dearly? On this premise, Jesus dedicated his entire life to do God's will and he calls us to do the same.

Jesus based his call on the logic of faith. Any response to his call hinges on our knowledge of God and his love. The ultimate question concerning the acceptance of this passage is this: Do we believe God is the creator and ruler of the universe? If we do, then this call makes sense; if we do not, it seems foolish. The extent to which we believe, but have doubts, is the extent to which we will have anxiety over Jesus' message.

Clearly, Jesus made a promise that he expected his followers to put to the test. Many Christians have ever done so, throwing in their lot completely with Christ. One such believer was Dietrich Bonhoeffer, a Lutheran pastor who lived in Hitler's Germany. He wrote:

"Be not anxious for the morrow." This is not to be taken as the philosophy of life or a moral law: It is the gospel of Jesus Christ, and only so can it be understood. Only those who follow him and know him can receive this word as a promise of the love of his Father and as a deliverance from the thraldom of material things. It is no care that frees the disciples from care, but their faith in Jesus

Christ . . . . It is senseless to pretend that we can make provision because we cannot alter the circumstances of this
world. Only God can take care, for it is he who rules the
world. (*The Cost of Discipleship*, 17)

Treasuring the care that God had for him above his own safety
and material well-being, Bonhoeffer resisted Nazi oppression and
was executed in 1945.

"Lord, give us the boldness of faith to trust our lives
completely and unwaveringly into your loving hands."

Matthew 7:1-6

1 "Judge not, that you be not judged. 2 For with the judgment
you pronounce you will be judged, and the measure you give will
be the measure you get. 3 Why do you see the speck that is in your
brother's eye, but do not notice the log that is in your own eye? 4
Or how can you say to your brother, 'Let me take the speck out of
your eye,' when there is the log in your own eye? 5 You hypocrite,
first take the log out of your own eye, and then you will see clearly
to take the speck out of your brother's eye.
6 "Do not give dogs what is holy; and do not throw your pearls
before swine, lest they trample them under foot and turn to
attack you."

When we read admonitions like "Judge not" and, "Why do you see the speck that is in your brother's eye, but do not notice the log that is in your own eye?" (Matthew 7:1,3), it is easy to forget that Jesus was speaking to men and women who were eagerly seeking to share his life and experience the fulfillment of his promises. Jesus was addressing people whose hearts were stirred by his words, people whom he called "blessed," "salt of the earth," "light of the world"—people who wanted to live a godly life. These words are, in fact, a reflection on how to love God with one's whole heart and life and strength.

At the center of wholehearted love of God is faith. Jesus lovingly exhorted his hearers to examine the desires of their hearts; to cast aside worry and anxiety; to have faith; to trust in God's love and care. This is an entirely new way of life founded on faith in an all-loving, all-merciful Father. It mirrors a heart that treasures God's thoughts and desires above its own, that has ceased worrying and always striving to achieve out of its own strength.

We are all called to this new way of life, and joy is its hallmark. "Many yearn to enter into that same joy, knowing, as they do that 'you are saved by grace—not by human works' but by the will of God," said St. Polycarp (*Letter to the Philippians*, 1).

It is a way of life that requires an honest appraisal of one's self before God. To some degree, we are all "hypocrites" (Matthew 7:5). Jesus calls us to know ourselves; he longs to liberate us from self-deception. And it is in this honesty and self-knowledge that we can be set free from the tyranny of judging others. As we come to know our own faults, to have a godly perception of ourselves, we can begin to love others *despite* their faults. We are released from the driving need to reform others before we can love them.

In that freedom, we can be brothers and sisters to those around us. We can live at peace—content with who we are and with that to which we are called. Great joy and peace attend this freedom.

We do not, however, attain this freedom through our own strength. In the kingdom of God, grace is poured out continually to enable us to live as Jesus commands us. As we allow the Holy Spirit to search our hearts and heal us, we can be confident that he will teach us how to love.

Matthew 7:7-12

7 "Ask, and it will be given you; seek, and you will find; knock, and it will be opened to you. 8 For every one who asks receives, and he who seeks finds, and to him who knocks it will be opened. 9 Or what man of you, if his son asks him for bread, will give him a stone? 10 Or if he asks for a fish, will give him a serpent? 11 If you then, who are evil, know how to give good gifts to your children, how much more will your Father who is in heaven give good things to those who ask him! 12 So whatever you wish that men would do to you, do so to them; for this is the law and the prophets."

Have you ever prayed for something and then been disappointed because God did not answer your prayer in the way you had wanted? This is a common experience to most Christians and, as a result, we are sometimes perplexed by Jesus' promise that we shall receive if we but ask. This passage is more accurately translated: "Keep asking and it will be given; keep seeking and you will find; keep knocking and the door will be opened to you." Jesus teaches us to seek after God in prayer continually throughout our lives.

God wants to give us what we ask, particularly those things which will help us to know him, his life, and his love. Therefore, we must learn to pray according to his will and in keeping with his ultimate purpose for our lives. Such prayer requires self-examination. Are we praying for selfish gain or because we want to know God and his love? As we grow in Christian maturity, we will become more and more at one with God's mind. We will find that *his* desires are becoming *our* desires.

A life of prayer brings us ever more deeply into the heart and mind of God. He wants to speak to our innermost hearts about his love for us. Too often we reduce God's desire to a process in which we seek favors and he either grants or denies them. God wants us to have a love relationship with him in which we know that every prayer will be heard and answered. We should expect answers to our prayers.

Jesus—who spent his life in prayer—is our model. When the time of his passion came, he asked the Father if his divine plan could be changed. When Jesus realized that God's divine plan for our salvation was not to be changed, he submitted himself to it completely. This was no easy task; Jesus agonized in prayer in the garden. But as the Holy Spirit conformed Jesus' human mind to the Father's perfect plan, he was able to accept the cross with joy.

"Father, assure us of your desire for us to know you, your life, your love. Help us to expect answers to our prayers, and to submit our wills to your perfect will."

Matthew 7:13-20

[13] "Enter by the narrow gate; for the gate is wide and the way is easy, that leads to destruction, and those who enter by it are many. [14] For the gate is narrow and the way is hard, that leads to life, and those who find it are few. [15] "Beware of false prophets, who come to you in sheep's clothing but inwardly are ravenous wolves. [16] You will know them by their fruits. Are grapes gathered from thorns, or figs from thistles? [17] So, every sound tree bears good fruit, but the bad tree bears evil fruit. [18] A sound tree cannot bear evil fruit, nor can a bad tree bear good fruit. [19] Every tree that does not bear good fruit is cut down and thrown into the fire. [20] Thus you will know them by their fruits."

As we near the end of the Sermon on the Mount, we are challenged to examine whether or not we are allowing Jesus and the words he taught to affect our lives. Are we bearing sufficient and appropriate fruit? Twice in these six verses, Jesus used the same words: "You will know them by their fruits" (Matthew 7:16,20). The word "fruit," from the Greek word *karpos*, means more than just an end product, the inevitable outcome of growth. The Greek word carries an implication of the *necessity* or *obligation* to bear fruit.

A true conversion to Jesus Christ presupposes a changed life, changed habit patterns, new sentiments, fruit borne because the believer is now grafted into Christ. And the good vine always bears good fruit. A desire to be fruitful is not necessarily enough to produce fruit. Often we want to bear good fruit, even while saying "no" to being one with Christ. We fail to realize that the crucial element in bearing fruit is union with Christ: "I am the vine, you are the branches. He who abides in me, and I in him, he it is that bears much fruit, for apart from me you can do nothing" (John 15:5).

All creation testifies to God's super-abundant life expressed in fruit-bearing: Buds become flowers; trees produce leaves; animals bear their young. None of these things happens independently of God's action, or just because people desire them. Nature testifies to the *karpos*, the necessity of becoming part of God's life and cooperating in order to bear fruit for his glory.

Of all created beings, humans alone can choose (by their free will) to bear good or evil fruit, to be a channel of God's life or a channel of death and decay. The ultimate choice is a personal one, but God the Father so wants us to be branches of the vine, that he sent his only begotten Son to redeem us. Jesus is now seated at the right hand of the throne of God, interceding for us. He is pouring out grace in order that we might choose his life. And he says: "By this my Father is glorified, that you bear much fruit, and so prove to be my disciples" (John 15:8).

"God, our Father, thank you for the glories of your creation, and for the privilege of participating with you in the process of bringing forth new life. You have given us everything we need in the person of your Son, Jesus Christ. Give us the grace, through the Holy Spirit, to bear fruit for your kingdom. We want to choose you today."

Matthew 7:21-29

[21] "Not every one who says to me, 'Lord, Lord,' shall enter the kingdom of heaven, but he who does the will of my Father who is in heaven. [22] On that day many will say to me, 'Lord, Lord, did we not prophesy in your name, and cast out demons in your name, and do many mighty works in your name?' [23] And then will I declare to them, 'I never knew you; depart from me, you evildoers.'

[24] "Every one then who hears these words of mine and does them will be like a wise man who built his house upon the rock; [25] and the rain fell, and the floods came, and the winds blew and beat upon that house, but it did not fall, because it had been founded on the rock. [26] And every one who hears these words of mine and does not do them will be like a foolish man who built his house upon the sand; [27] and the rain fell, and the floods came, and the winds blew and beat against that house, and it fell; and great was the fall of it."

[28] And when Jesus finished these sayings, the crowds were astonished at his teaching, [29] for he taught them as one who had authority, and not as their scribes.

Jesus concluded his Sermon on the Mount with the parable of the wise man and the fool. The parable presents us with a choice: To hear God's word and act upon it, or to hear God's word and reject it for worldly wisdom. Either way, God's word demands a response from us. We are invited to follow Christ and to found our lives on him as our rock: "Trust in the LORD forever, for the LORD GOD is an everlasting rock" (Isaiah 26:4).

Through Christ's great love for us, we *can* respond to this invitation. The psalmist chose to base his life on the Lord as his rock, knowing that the Lord's love endures forever (Psalm 118:1). The psalmist was not afraid of the forces of evil around him (118:6). With the Lord as his refuge, he proclaimed: "The LORD is my strength and my might; he has become my salvation" (118:14).

God's love is unconditional and eternal. He stands as a rock, the foundation of our security and protection. God made his love known to us through Jesus Christ, but we need to respond to him in order to receive the fullness of what he offers. God's unfailing love will draw us to Jesus Christ and enable us to build our foundation on him. "Those of steadfast mind you keep in peace—in peace because they trust in you" (Isaiah 26:3).

Mother Teresa of Calcutta, drawn by God's love, has founded her life on him. She urges us to accept God's love and to choose him:

"Let's believe in God's love and let's be faithful to him. If you look at the cross, you shall see his head lowered to kiss you. You will see his arms stretched out to embrace you. You will see his heart open to welcome you. Don't be afraid. He loves us, and he wants us to love one another. He loves us in spite of how poor and sinful we are. His love is true and we should believe in his love." (*One Heart Full of Love*)

"Lord Jesus, we believe in your great love for us. In response to that love, we want to found our lives on you, for in you we have found an everlasting rock."

Jesus' Miraculous Works

MATTHEW
8–9

Matthew 8:1-4

1   When he came down from the mountain, great crowds followed him; 2 and behold, a leper came to him and knelt before him, saying, "Lord, if you will, you can make me clean." 3 And he stretched out his hand and touched him, saying, "I will; be clean." And immediately his leprosy was cleansed. 4 And Jesus said to him, "See that you say nothing to any one; but go, show yourself to the priest, and offer the gift that Moses commanded, for a proof to the people."

A s we read through the Gospel of Matthew, we come to see the dual nature of Jesus' mission—his "words" and his "works." Jesus had spoken on the mountain (Matthew 5–7) as the new Moses, revealing to the people through his teaching how he was the fulfillment of the law and the prophets. He spoke with authority and his listeners were astonished by his teaching. Now he was on his way to Capernaum to work among the people in Galilee (8:1–11:1). The healing of the leper is the first miracle in a series of ten (8:1–9:34) that revealed Jesus' power and love.

These miracles were meant as signs of the reality of the kingdom of God. By his works, Jesus showed his power over the forces of evil. His miracles had spiritual significance intended both to reveal to the people who he was and to draw them to him. They were visible manifestations of the new life that was available to all who would open their hearts to him. "Jesus . . . manifested his glory; and his disciples believed in him" (John 2:11).

We, too, need to be examining the impact of Jesus' words and works in our lives. This is the way we are strengthened in our faith. God the Father wants us to come to a deeper knowledge of his Son, no matter what the condition of our spiritual understanding; it is a revelation of the love of God that "surpasses knowledge" (Ephesians 3:19), made possible through the indwelling Spirit.

God wants us to approach Jesus as the leper did: "A leper came to him and knelt before him saying, 'Lord, if you will, you can make me clean.' And he stretched out his hand and touched him, saying, 'I will' " (Matthew 8:2-3). As we read through this cycle of miracles, let us ask the Holy Spirit to reveal to us more deeply who Jesus is and what he wants to do in our lives.

"Holy Spirit of God, teach us who Jesus is and help us to understand how he wants to work in our lives and use us. Let our faith deepen and grow and help us to respond to Jesus."

Matthew 8:5-13

5   As he entered Capernaum, a centurion came forward to him, beseeching him 6 and saying, "Lord, my servant is lying paralyzed at home, in terrible distress." 7 And he said to him, "I will come and heal him." 8 But the centurion answered him, "Lord, I am not worthy to have you come under my roof; but only say the word, and my servant will be healed. 9 For I am a man under authority, with soldiers under me; and I say to one, 'Go,' and he goes, and to another, 'Come,' and he comes, and to my slave, 'Do this,' and he does it." 10 When Jesus heard him, he marveled, and said to those who followed him, "Truly, I say to you, not even in Israel have I found such faith. 11 I tell you, many will come from east and west and sit at table with Abraham, Isaac, and Jacob in the kingdom of heaven, 12 while the sons of the kingdom will be thrown into the outer darkness; there men will weep and gnash their teeth." 13 And to the centurion Jesus said, "Go; be it done for you as you have believed." And the servant was healed at that very moment.

I am a man under authority. (Matthew 8:9)

The centurion was a man who understood authority. He was both subject to authority and had soldiers under his authority (Matthew 8:9). He knew what this meant: He was to obey those in positions of legitimate authority over him, and he could expect obedience from those under his authority.

This understanding opened the centurion to the great faith that he displayed in Jesus. By comprehending the authority that the Father had given to Jesus, there was no doubt in the centurion's mind that Jesus could heal his servant. For the centurion, Jesus didn't even have to be physically present in order for the servant to be healed. By his authority, Jesus only had to "say the word" (Matthew 8:8), and the servant was healed.

How do we understand the authority of God? We know that God created the world and has given us dominion over it (Genesis 1:26). We also know that the Father has given Jesus "all authority in heaven and on earth" (Matthew 28:18), and has put him at the head of the body, the church (Colossians 1:18). Therefore, all authority on earth is ultimately derived from God. Jesus reminded Pontius Pilate of this during his passion: "You would have no power over me unless it had been given you from above" (John 19:11).

From time to time over the years, we may have been disappointed in human authority, especially as we have seen it used inappropriately. God, however, never tries to control us with his authority. He has given us the freedom to choose good or evil. When we recognize God's perfect authority, we will be more likely to want to obey the laws he has given us through the church. They are a gift intended to help us live more loving and fruitful lives—lives that will bear witness to his goodness and love.

Like the centurion, an acknowledgement of God's authority over us can open us to greater faith. When we pray in the name of Jesus, we are invoking his authority over all things, including fear, sickness, anxiety, and sin. Although we are "not worthy," Jesus is pleased with the faith we display when we call on him in times of distress. Like the centurion, we can have great confidence in the power of Jesus.

Matthew 8:14-17

¹⁴ And when Jesus entered Peter's house, he saw his mother-in-law lying sick with a fever; ¹⁵ he touched her hand, and the fever left her, and she rose and served him. ¹⁶ That evening they brought to him many who were possessed with demons; and he cast out the spirits with a word, and healed all who were sick. ¹⁷ This was to fulfil what was spoken by the prophet Isaiah, "He took our infirmities and bore our diseases."

Have you ever felt some mornings that you just couldn't get out of bed? Perhaps something you dreaded was scheduled to happen that day. It may have been a job evaluation, another day of a prolonged illness, or the necessity of caring for a sick or cranky child.

Like Peter's mother-in-law, who was bedridden and feverish, we too can be weighed down by physical, emotional, or spiritual burdens. During these times of infirmity, we can become depressed, making it almost impossible for us to love and care for others. It can even become difficult to believe that God (or anyone else) cares about us.

When Jesus heard about Peter's mother-in-law, he took her by the hand and healed her. Immediately, the fever left, and she began to serve Jesus and his disciples. What power, authority and love are manifest in Jesus' presence! There is nothing—no illness, no sin, no demon—that can stand against him.

Matthew told this story to show how Jesus exercised his authority through love. He loves us so much that he became a man and entered into our weak and wounded condition, triumphing over it by giving up his own life on the cross. He took on our infirmities and endured our pain. Now he invites us to receive his love and healing power. "He heals the brokenhearted, and binds up their wounds" (Psalm 147:3). Jesus wants to heal us in the deepest way possible—by increasing our capacity to accept in faith all that he did for us on the cross, by drawing us into an ever-closer union with him.

Ever striving to be like his Master, St. Paul sought to become all things to all people (1 Corinthians 9:22). When we believe in Jesus, partake of his mysteries at the altar, and keep his commandments, the Spirit enters into us more deeply and gives us the power to reflect Jesus' love more fully. Jesus wants to rule our activities through his Spirit, moving us to love the Lord and to serve his people with humility and compassion (see *Catechism of the Catholic Church*, 2084).

Strengthened by the presence of the Spirit in us, let us walk in the authority and compassion of Jesus. As we do, we too will receive the ability to become all things to all people, serving them in love.

Matthew 8:18-22

18 Now when Jesus saw great crowds around him, he gave orders to go over to the other side. 19 And a scribe came up and said to him, "Teacher, I will follow you wherever you go." 20 And Jesus said to him, "Foxes have holes, and birds of the air have nests; but the Son of man has nowhere to lay his head." 21 Another of the disciples said to him, "Lord, let me first go and bury my father." 22 But Jesus said to him, "Follow me, and leave the dead to bury their own dead."

In these short dialogues, Jesus was emphasizing the importance of following him and describing some of the ramifications of doing so. In addition, he also gave a veiled reference to who he was. Those who had ears to hear would come to understand through this small incident that Jesus was revealing himself to be the long-awaited Messiah.

The first disciple, a scribe who professed himself willing to forsake all for Jesus, was acting impulsively. Jesus recognized the condition of his heart and knew that his initial fervor would be short-lived. He therefore suggested to the man just what his commitment might entail (Matthew 8:19-20). The second disciple seemed willing to follow Jesus but had other business to attend to first, indicating that his call to discipleship was not his highest priority. Jesus urged him not to allow concerns for things of the world to cloud his perceptions of the kingdom of God. By putting God's will first, he would insure that his family would not be neglected (8:21-22).

As he began to reveal himself, Jesus used the phrase "Son of man" to describe himself (Matthew 8:20). This title is found in the gospels about seventy times. On the one hand, it meant "man," that is, a son of Adam, and emphasized man's smallness before God (see Psalm 8:4). On the other hand, "Son of man" described an eternal king whom all nations would serve; not just a savior, but a heavenly savior. "There came one like a Son of man, and he came to the Ancient of Days and was presented before him. And to him was given dominion and glory and kingdom, that all peoples, nations, and languages should serve him" (Daniel 7:13-14). In Jewish apocalyptic writings, the title described a person endowed with glorious power, one who would come at the end of time to rule the kingdom of God.

By using "Son of man," Jesus was beginning to reveal himself, even though his revelation remained somewhat veiled. To those who listened to him without faith, he was describing himself as a man. But to those whose hearts were open, he was announcing the arrival of the long-awaited Messiah.

Matthew 8:23-27

²³ And when he got into the boat, his disciples followed him.
²⁴ And behold, there arose a great storm on the sea, so that the boat
was being swamped by the waves; but he was asleep. ²⁵ And they
went and woke him, saying, "Save, Lord; we are perishing." ²⁶ And
he said to them, "Why are you afraid, O men of little faith?" Then
he rose and rebuked the winds and the sea; and there was a great
calm. ²⁷ And the men marveled, saying, "What sort of man is this,
that even winds and sea obey him?"

The account in Matthew's gospel of Jesus calming the storm
continued the flow of miracle stories begun earlier with the
healing of a leper (Matthew 8:1-17). The storm episode
intensified the disciples' wonder at Jesus' authority: "What sort of
man is this, that even the winds and sea obey him?" (8:27).
Together, these events were a dramatic revelation of Jesus, the
Messiah, inaugurating the kingdom of God.

This incident tied the miracles into the theme of discipleship,
which runs through this section of Matthew. In the preceding
scene, immediately after Jesus' emphasis on the dedication
required to follow him (Matthew 8:18-22), the "disciples followed" Jesus into the boat (8:23). By following him, they were trying to live as genuine disciples, but their faith evaporated as the
wind rose and fear overcame them.

This story doubles as a teaching about how believers should
not lose faith in times of crisis. It leads to a cycle in which the
author contrasts miracle accounts with teaching on discipleship

(Matthew 8:28–9:38). The counterpoint pattern sheds light on Jesus' message that mature faith goes beyond believing in miracles to trusting in Jesus.

The Greek word (*seismos*) describing the storm that rocked the disciples' boat (Matthew 8:24) is the same word used elsewhere in Matthew (and the New Testament) to describe the upheaval and calamity to occur in the end times, when tribulation will shake the church (24:7; Mark 13:8). Use of this word for the storm helped early Christian readers to realize that they must not let themselves be immobilized by persecution and adversity.

The story of the storm serves as a bridge uniting Matthew's community with us. Peter's boat represents the church being tossed on the world's precarious waters. Fearful and overwhelmed, the disciples cried, "Lord, save us," echoing the prayer found in even ancient liturgies, *Kyrie, eleison*: "Lord, have mercy." The Messiah asks every generation, "Why are you afraid, O men of little faith?" Like the apostles, we do have faith, but it is immature and easily shaken. Jesus invites us to grow in faith and to experience his saving power.

"Lord, we pray that our faith will grow and deepen. We pray for the church and all her members that we would trust that you are sufficient for all our needs."

Matthew 8:28-34

28 And when he came to the other side, to the country of the Gadarenes, two demoniacs met him, coming out of the tombs, so fierce that no one could pass that way. 29 And behold, they cried out, "What have you to do with us, O Son of God? Have you come here to torment us before the time?" 30 Now a herd of many swine was feeding at some distance from them. 31 And the demons begged him, "If you cast us out, send us away into the herd of swine." 32 And he said to them, "Go." So they came out and went into the swine; and behold, the whole herd rushed down the steep bank into the sea, and perished in the waters. 33 The herdsmen fled, and going into the city they told everything, and what had happened to the demoniacs. 34 And behold, all the city came out to meet Jesus; and when they saw him, they begged him to leave their neighborhood.

Gadara was a city east of the Jordan River in the non-Jewish region of the Decapolis. Even here, in pagan territory, Jesus demonstrated his awesome power and authority. The demons recognized and feared Jesus' power (Matthew 8:29), even though the "appointed time" had not yet come when he would conquer Satan by dying and rising to life.

Jesus permitted the demons to enter into the swine, which then rushed into the sea and were drowned. All who watched were astonished and raced to tell the townspeople what had happened. We might expect this great miracle to heal the people's unbelief. Instead, they became fearful of Jesus and "begged him to leave their neighborhood" (Matthew 8:34). This attitude may puzzle us at first until we realize that sometimes we have the same reaction. God has shown his power and love in our midst many times, yet there are times when we still respond by turning our hearts away. In these times, we too are asking Jesus to leave.

Jesus wants us to experience cleansing and freedom from sins such as self-centeredness, anger, deception, and lust. Through his love, God will bring these areas to light in our lives and show us more clearly our need to change these areas and be healed. As our eyes are opened, we can then decide whether we will allow Jesus to make us whole or whether we will resist his work.

Fear is the single most important factor that causes us to turn our hearts away from God; fear of change or fear of the unknown can paralyze us. We can become so comfortable with our lives just as they are, with all their sins and problems, that we forget God's desire that we become one with him in Jesus Christ. Jesus died on the cross to release us from these fears. He wants to bring us to the fullness of the relationship we once had with the Father. Let us hold on to the truth that God has a great plan for our lives.

"Lord Jesus, you have destroyed the power of darkness and all the chains that hold us in bondage. Send your Holy Spirit to enlighten my mind and show me the fullness of life that you offer to all your people."

Matthew 9:1-8

1 And getting into a boat he crossed over and came to his own city. 2 And behold, they brought to him a paralytic, lying on his bed; and when Jesus saw their faith he said to the paralytic, "Take heart, my son; your sins are forgiven." 3 And behold, some of the scribes said to themselves, "This man is blaspheming." 4 But Jesus, knowing their thoughts, said, "Why do you think evil in your hearts? 5 For which is easier, to say, 'Your sins are forgiven,' or to say, 'Rise and walk'? 6 But that you may know that the Son of man has authority on earth to forgive sins"—he then said to the paralytic—'Rise, take up your bed and go home." 7 And he rose and went home. 8 When the crowds saw it, they were afraid, and they glorified God, who had given such authority to men.

After reading the accounts of ten miracles in just two chapters (Matthew 8:1–9:38), we might be surprised to learn that healing was *not* Matthew's central concern in relating these accounts. More central to his purpose was to show that Jesus is the Messiah who had come to free the world of sin and darkness through his cross and to usher in the kingdom of God. Without this saving work, there is no forgiveness of sins; without the forgiveness of sins, there is no healing.

The paralyzed man actually experienced two kinds of healing—physical and spiritual. Both are signs of the coming kingdom, when the Son of man will complete his work of healing and restoration. But clearly, there is a connection between the two healings, for Jesus confirmed his power to forgive sins by demonstrating his ability to heal.

Critics of the Bible often try to discredit healing stories because they don't see any connection between physical healing and spiritual forces, either good or evil. Most of us would not attribute *all* sickness to the work of demons, or *all* healing to a miraculous work of God. Nevertheless, sickness and disorder were unleashed in God's perfect world at the dawn of history when sin entered the world. Doctors continue to find, even today, that a multitude of factors outside the physical realm, including prayer, can have an impact on one's ability to heal. This should make us pause before rejecting healing through spiritual means as a primitive religious concept. Miracles show that reality is open to God's transforming power.

The crowd was not just amazed at Jesus' miracle (as in Mark 2:1-12); they were struck by the fact that God had given such authority to human beings. Matthew would have us ponder this truth (as he and the early community of believers undoubtedly had done) and consider it in light of what has been revealed about Jesus as the Messiah of word and deed. Truly, this Jesus should be taken seriously.

"Lord Jesus, you know how much healing is needed in our lives. Open our hearts and free us that we might allow you to work in us and heal us. May we come to know that you truly are the promised Messiah who has inaugurated the kingdom of God."

Matthew 9:9-13

9 As Jesus passed on from there, he saw a man called Matthew sitting at the tax office; and he said to him, "Follow me." And he rose and followed him.

10 And as he sat at table in the house, behold, many tax collectors and sinners came and sat down with Jesus and his disciples. 11 And when the Pharisees saw this, they said to his disciples, "Why does your teacher eat with tax collectors and sinners?" 12 But when he heard it, he said, "Those who are well have no need of a physician, but those who are sick. 13 Go and learn what this means, 'I desire mercy, and not sacrifice.' For I came not to call the righteous, but sinners."

Matthew was an outcast—a Jew who served the financial arm of the Roman Empire that occupied Palestine. He was probably aware that in many ways he had betrayed his people and made accommodations with the pagan culture that held them in subjection. Still, when Jesus called, Matthew left everything behind and followed him (Matthew 9:9).

It was Matthew's awareness of his condition that enabled him to respond so readily to the Lord. Matthew knew he was sinful: He was probably reminded of it every day as he endured the scornful looks and bitter words that his own people directed at him and his form of livelihood. Perhaps he also followed the common practice among tax collectors of over-charging his clients and keeping the extra money for himself (see Luke 3:12-13). Whatever the case, Matthew knew he needed a savior.

Imagine Matthew's hope and joy when he heard Jesus say, "Those who are well have no need of a physician, but those who are sick . . . For I came not to call the righteous, but sinners" (Matthew 9:12,13). This is the wonder of our God: He calls us while we are still sinners (see Romans 5:8). Matthew knew that he was spiritually sick and in great need. This knowledge could have influenced him to abandon his old life and follow Jesus, the only one who could heal him.

The popular view in the world is that we are basically good people. Despite the popularity of this notion, we should be certain of one thing: We have all been wounded by original sin (see Romans 3:10-12, 23). We all seek after our own needs and desires before we think about the desires of the Lord (see 7:15, 17-20). When Matthew realized this, he forsook his cherished possessions and ideas and followed Jesus. The same can also be true for us. If we ask him, the Holy Spirit will not only show us our sin, he will speak words of comfort and hope to us, calling us to Jesus, our great healer.

"Lord Jesus, you came to redeem and heal the sinful. By your Spirit, may I experience your work in my life and learn to follow you."

Matthew 9:14-17

[14] Then the disciples of John came to him, saying, "Why do we and the Pharisees fast, but your disciples do not fast?" [15] And Jesus said to them, "Can the wedding guests mourn as long as the bridegroom is with them? The days will come, when the bridegroom is taken away from them, and then they will fast. [16] And no one puts a piece of unshrunk cloth on an old garment, for the patch tears away from the garment, and a worse tear is made. [17] Neither is new wine put into old wineskins; if it is, the skins burst, and the wine is spilled, and the skins are destroyed; but new wine is put into fresh wineskins, and so both are preserved."

Something new was happening through Jesus: A new order was beginning and the old was passing away. Jesus described this new relationship with God using various images. He said, for example, that it was like a wedding feast where the guests rejoiced in the presence of the bridegroom (Matthew 9:15). In this veiled way, Jesus was teaching the people that he was the bridegroom. His presence fulfilled the Old Testament prophecies that God would forgive his people and join himself to them as through a marriage covenant (see Hosea 2:18-20; Isaiah 62:4-5).

The parables of the wineskins and the patched cloth illustrate the newness of what was happening. Jesus creates things anew; he doesn't merely patch them up. New wine is the sign of a new era: Jesus is the one who dispenses the new wine. Christ came to renew the whole universe. This renewal began at his birth, was fulfilled in his death and resurrection, and will be perfected in his second coming.

The body of Christ reflects the new order established by Christ and is a sign of Jesus' presence among his people. It is to reflect to the world the love, harmony, peace, and unity that come from Christ. Jesus wants his body on earth to mirror the love and unity he shares with his Father and the Holy Spirit. But this is hardly possible when his followers are divided and at odds with one another.

As Christians, we should be keenly aware of our responsibility to pray for unity among Christian churches according to the mind and heart of Christ. Disunity and division in our own time prevent the fulfillment of the new reality Jesus inaugurated in his death and resurrection. We pray for unity so that the work of Christ will be fulfilled. The bridegroom cannot rejoice fully when he sees division among the very people he came to gather together.

"Lord Jesus, we pray that all Christians might be united according to your mind and heart. Send us your Holy Spirit to teach us to repent for our suspicion, anger, and pride. Make us one, Lord, that all the world may see the new life you came to establish."

Matthew 9:18-26

18 While he was thus speaking to them, behold, a ruler came in and knelt before him, saying, "My daughter has just died; but come and lay your hand on her, and she will live." 19 And Jesus rose and followed him, with his disciples. 20 And behold, a woman who had suffered from a hemorrhage for twelve years came up behind him and touched the fringe of his garment; 21 for she said to herself, "If I only touch his garment, I shall be made well." 22 Jesus turned, and seeing her he said, "Take heart, daughter; your faith has made you well." And instantly the woman was made well. 23 And when Jesus came to the ruler's house, and saw the flute players, and the crowd making a tumult, 24 he said, "Depart; for the girl is not dead but sleeping." And they laughed at him. 25 But when the crowd had been put outside, he went in and took her by the hand, and the girl arose. 26 And the report of this went through all that district.

In these two stories, Matthew shows how a variety of people responded to Jesus. A man of considerable eminence in his own town came and fell at his feet, asking him to come and heal his daughter. As they were proceeding to the man's home, a hemorrhaging woman came forward and fell at his feet, confessing that she was healed just by touching the hem of Jesus' garment. Finally, the people from the ruler's household showed no faith in Jesus, even to the point of mocking and laughing at him.

How do we look at Jesus? Is he some wonder worker of the past? Was he perhaps a very holy man, an outstanding combination of generosity and humility? How deeply do we believe that

Jesus Christ is the eternal Son of God, our perfect and complete salvation? Many of our attitudes about faith and the Christian life are formed by our culture, and if we look around, it becomes clear to us that this world functions with little recourse to faith. Yet, it is in this environment that our thoughts about God are formed.

When we act out of envy or bitterness, does this not signify a lack of faith? Are we not saying, "I have a right to be angry because nobody (not even God) is looking after my interests"? When we repent of a specific sin, but resign ourselves to the fact that we will probably go ahead and commit it again, is this not a sign that we lack faith in the power of the blood to cleanse us and free us from sin? When we become restless during our reading of scripture or prayer time, is it because we don't expect Jesus to speak to us and give us peace and joy in his presence?

These are but a few of the many ways in which our unbelief manifests itself. Jesus wants us to put aside thoughts like these so that our faith can become more like that of the ruler and the hemorrhaging woman. He wants to tell us: "Do not fear, only believe" (Mark 5:36). He can say this only if we have begun to put off our old attitudes and mind sets and to ask him to give us a new mind formed in his image. Let us come before God in humility and ask him to increase our faith. Let us beg the Holy Spirit to fill us with an abiding faith and trust. Let us touch the hem of his garment today.

Matthew 9:27-31

²⁷ And as Jesus passed on from there, two blind men followed him, crying aloud, "Have mercy on us, Son of David." ²⁸ When he entered the house, the blind men came to him; and Jesus said to them, "Do you believe that I am able to do this?" They said to him, "Yes, Lord." ²⁹ Then he touched their eyes, saying, "According to your faith be it done to you." ³⁰ And their eyes were opened. And Jesus sternly charged them, "See that no one knows it." ³¹ But they went away and spread his fame through all that district.

Isaiah told of a time when, out of gloom and darkness, the eyes of the blind would see (Isaiah 29:18). This prophecy of blindness being cured is characteristic of messianic literature. When John the Baptist sent his disciples to Jesus to ask him if he were the Messiah, Jesus replied: "Go and tell John what you hear and see: the blind receive their sight and the lame walk, lepers are cleansed and the deaf hear, and the dead are raised up, and the poor have the good news preached to them" (Matthew 11:4-5).

Jesus *is* the Messiah, the promised one spoken of in the Old Testament, whom God sent to save his people. When the two blind men cried out to Jesus to have mercy on them, Jesus asked if they believed he could heal them (Matthew 9:28). The word Jesus used for belief is (in Greek) *pistis*, which means faith. *Pistis* is faith that comes from intelligent adherence, not a leap in the dark.

For the blind men, having *pistis* would have involved knowing the prophecies about the coming Messiah and being able to measure Jesus' words and deeds against these predictions. In essence,

Jesus was asking the men if they believed that he was the Messiah, the Son of God. Their physical healing came about as a result of their act of faith (Matthew 9:29).

Jesus wants to prove to us that he is the fulfillment of all the Old Testament related about the coming Messiah. We should look at the Old Testament evidence and compare that to what we know about Jesus. Then, ask him to give us the faith to believe. The extent to which we can say, "I believe," is the extent to which we will experience God's love and power in our lives.

"Lord Jesus, we believe that you are the promised Messiah and that you came to raise us to a new living hope. Open our eyes of faith, as you opened the eyes of the blind men that we may see you more clearly. Make us eager to tell others how you have worked in our lives, so that all may come to know you, the Messiah."

Matthew 9:32-38

³² As they were going away, behold, a dumb demoniac was brought to him. ³³ And when the demon had been cast out, the dumb man spoke; and the crowds marveled, saying, "Never was anything like this seen in Israel." ³⁴ But the Pharisees said, "He casts out demons by the prince of demons."

³⁵ And Jesus went about all the cities and villages, teaching in their synagogues and preaching the gospel of the kingdom, and healing every disease and every infirmity. ³⁶ When he saw the crowds, he had compassion for them, because they were harassed and helpless, like sheep without a shepherd. ³⁷ Then he said to his disciples, "The harvest is plentiful, but the laborers are few; ³⁸ pray therefore the Lord of the harvest to send out laborers into his harvest."

Jesus came to inaugurate the eternal, unshakable kingdom of God. He looked on the multitudes with compassion and great mercy (Matthew 9:36). He saw the people wandering aimlessly; their passions and desires drove them and they acted without purpose or meaning in their lives. Many were crippled by fears, unbelief, and the lies of Satan. Despite all this, Jesus knew the love that the Father has for each and every person. As a reflection of this love, he went about "preaching the gospel of the kingdom and healing every disease and every infirmity" (9:35).

In the kingdom of God, Jesus reigns as Lord and King. Those who have embraced the kingdom know who they are and who their king is. They have confidence in their king and his love for them. He is their light, their comfort (2 Corinthians 1:3-4), and their strength (Psalm 28:7-8). Their desire is to love and serve God.

Jesus' healing of the demoniac is another sign that he wants to heal us all, so that we may share in the life of the Father. He wants to show us the ways in which our bondage to sin keeps us from witnessing to God's glory in our lives. This healing—the last in a series of ten showing Jesus as the Messiah of deed as well as word (Matthew 8:1–9:38)—is another sign of the work of healing the Messiah of God wants to do in all our lives.

The Pharisees saw what Jesus was doing, but insisted that he was in league with the devil and derived his power from the evil one (Matthew 9:34). Even in this early part of Jesus' ministry, we see signs of the clash that would take him to Jerusalem to suffer and die. Even so, Jesus continued on with his mission and invited his disciples to go as laborers into the harvest (Matthew 9:37-38).

In the words of Mother Teresa: "Jesus did not stop his works of charity because the Pharisees and others hated him or tried to spoil His Father's work. He just went about doing good" (*Total Surrender*, p.150). We too, embracing Jesus as the Messiah in our lives, are called as the body of Christ to work together to further the kingdom by announcing the good news and leading others by word and action to Jesus and the salvation he offers.

The Missionary Discourse

MATTHEW
10

Matthew 10:1-7

1 And he called to him his twelve disciples and gave them authority over unclean spirits, to cast them out, and to heal every disease and every infirmity. 2 The names of the twelve apostles are these: first, Simon, who is called Peter, and Andrew his brother; James the son of Zebedee, and John his brother; 3 Philip and Bartholomew; Thomas and Matthew the tax collector; James the son of Alphaeus, and Thaddaeus; 4 Simon the Cananaean, and Judas Iscariot, who betrayed him.
5 These twelve Jesus sent out, charging them, "Go nowhere among the Gentiles, and enter no town of the Samaritans, 6 but go rather to the lost sheep of the house of Israel. 7 And preach as you go, saying, 'The kingdom of heaven is at hand.'" ▨▨▨

"The kingdom of heaven is at hand." (Matthew 10:7)

The apostles had been in the company of Jesus as he traveled around the Galilean countryside proclaiming the good news of the kingdom, curing every disease and affliction (Matthew 9:35). Now Jesus was sending them out as his ambassadors to gain firsthand experience as missionaries. In commissioning them, he empowered them to heal as he had healed, to cast out demons as he had cast them out, to proclaim, as he had, that the kingdom of God was at hand (Matthew 10:1,7).

These quite ordinary men, with little of what our world deems necessary for success—education, wealth, social standing—were chosen by Jesus to carry on his work. These were the ones who gathered in prayer after his ascension and—after the coming of the Holy Spirit at Pentecost—preached and baptized so that three thousand were added to their number (Acts 2:41). They remained faithful to their calling, for "every day in the temple and at home they did not cease teaching and preaching Jesus as the Christ," despite the persecutions they endured (5:42).

The apostles' mission is not an exclusive one. By our baptism, we too are commissioned to follow in the footsteps of Jesus and preach the message of salvation. Like the apostles, we are empowered by the Holy Spirit to proclaim the good news of Jesus Christ. There is a whole world of people for whom Jesus shed his saving blood but who (because the gospel has not touched their lives) will not experience its elevating and perfecting power in their societies and cultures or in their personal lives.

If we are faithful to our calling as ministers of Christ's word, the gospel *will* be spread and God's kingdom *will* be built. Today, let us pray particularly for all clergy that they might know the truth and power of Jesus. May they see his power manifested in their ministry and remain faithful to their responsibility to proclaim the gospel message. Let us pray also that we may faithfully and generously do our part in carrying on the mission of Jesus.

"Lord Jesus, the good news is that the kingdom of God is at hand. May all those called and ordained to serve you know your life and power more deeply as they proclaim the gospel. Help us to be faithful to our call to share the good news."

Matthew 10:8-15

[8] "Heal the sick, raise the dead, cleanse lepers, cast out demons. You received without paying, give without pay. [9] Take no gold, nor silver, nor copper in your belts, [10] no bag for your journey, nor two tunics, nor sandals, nor a staff; for the laborer deserves his food. [11] And whatever town or village you enter, find out who is worthy in it, and stay with him until you depart. [12] As you enter the house, salute it. [13] And if the house is worthy, let your peace come upon it; but if it is not worthy, let your peace return to you. [14] And if any one will not receive you or listen to your words, shake off the dust from your feet as you leave that house or town. [15] Truly, I say to you, it shall be more tolerable on the day of judgment for the land of Sodom and Gomorrah than for that town."

Matthew's Gospel is not so much a history of past events as a theological interpretation of them. The author was providing guidance to his community and other Christian communities on the call of discipleship. As he was recalling Jesus' instructions to the twelve (when he sent them out on their first missionary journey), Matthew was fully aware of the great commission that applies to *all* believers: "Go therefore and make disciples of all nations" (Matthew 28:19). The mission given by Jesus to his disciples was unique, yet, as baptized Christians, we too participate in Jesus' great commission.

What are some of the implications of discipleship in preaching the good news? What was to be the attitude of heart among the twelve? There was to be confidence in the power of the gospel to change lives, to heal, to purify (Matthew 10:8). There was certainly an urgency about the mission. It was not to be delayed until "proper equipment" could be acquired (10:9-10). Nothing was to distract them from their mission. Subsistence, but not profit, was to be their expectation. Preaching the gospel was not to be a business, and it would not be accepted by all. Where it was rejected, the response was not to be condemnation or a desire for retribution; it was a symbolic shaking of the dust from their feet (10:14).

It is clear from Jesus' words that the apostles were to be totally reliant on God and his goodness and generosity. Such an attitude recognizes God as a loving and personal Father who will always faithfully provide for his people and will never abandon them. Such a loving Father will sustain us as well.

How different this way of thinking is from that which many of us have. We sometimes act as though God were miserly, begrudging of his love, not really caring for us. This mind-set affects and limits the power of the gospel message we preach. We can only have a true missionary's heart when we trust in God and are convinced of his generosity and faithfulness.

"Loving Father, we know you are faithful to your promises. We commit ourselves to living and preaching the good news of salvation through your Son Jesus through the power of the indwelling Holy Spirit. Keep us faithful to our promise as you are to yours."

Matthew 10:16-23

16 "Behold, I send you out as sheep in the midst of wolves; so be wise as serpents and innocent as doves. 17 Beware of men; for they will deliver you up to councils, and flog you in their synagogues, 18 and you will be dragged before governors and kings for my sake, to bear testimony before them and the Gentiles. 19 When they deliver you up, do not be anxious how you are to speak or what you are to say; for what you are to say will be given to you in that hour; 20 for it is not you who speak, but the Spirit of your Father speaking through you. 21 Brother will deliver up brother to death, and the father his child, and children will rise against parents and have them put to death; 22 and you will be hated by all for my name's sake. But he who endures to the end will be saved. 23 When they persecute you in one town, flee to the next; for truly, I say to you, you will not have gone through all the towns of Israel, before the Son of man comes."

The Gospel of Matthew is viewed by some scholars as the gospel to the Jews. Matthew's main purpose was to convince his Jewish readers that Jesus was the promised Messiah. His method was to show how Jesus' life and ministry fulfilled the Old Testament scriptures and prophecies about the Anointed One who was to come.

The primitive church experienced persecution from both Jews and Gentiles. Despite this, Jesus told his apostles that he was sending them out "as sheep in the midst of wolves" (Matthew 10:16). He warned them that it would not be easy to follow him and be his disciples. They would be persecuted—at times even by their own families who would not share their love of Christ or their desire to follow him.

Truly, the way of discipleship was not going to be easy, but Jesus did not leave them defenseless. He promised that the Holy Spirit would be with them, teaching them and guiding them in every situation. Jesus knew that if they were true to him and to his teaching, they would be "wise as serpents and innocent as doves" (Matthew 10:16). They would be innocent as doves because they would be free from judgmentalism and anger as the power of Christ's love transformed their hearts.

Sometimes we too may feel that we are going out among wolves. We may face ridicule or rejection because of our beliefs. People in the world may try to lure and entice us in order to show us how weak we are. The harassment we endure may tempt us to lash out at others or to write people off. At times, timidity may make us reluctant to live and share our faith.

Our protection and our wisdom will come from the Holy Spirit as we seek God through prayer and the grounding that comes as we read scripture and hear it proclaimed in the liturgy. If our minds are filled with the truth of God's word, we will have the strength and the knowledge to withstand those who oppose Christ and his way of life.

"Heavenly Father, thank you for your promise to teach us what is wise and good. Help us every day to love our enemies and to pray for those who assail us so that we may be witnesses that your Son truly lives."

Matthew 10:24-33

[24] "A disciple is not above his teacher, nor a servant above his master; [25] it is enough for the disciple to be like his teacher, and the servant like his master. If they have called the master of the house Beelzebul, how much more will they malign those of his household. [26] "So have no fear of them; for nothing is covered that will not be revealed, or hidden that will not be known. [27] What I tell you in the dark, utter in the light; and what you hear whispered, proclaim upon the housetops. [28] And do not fear those who kill the body but cannot kill the soul; rather fear him who can destroy both soul and body in hell. [29] Are not two sparrows sold for a penny? And not one of them will fall to the ground without your Father's will. [30] But even the hairs of your head are all numbered. [31] Fear not, therefore; you are of more value than many sparrows. [32] So every one who acknowledges me before men, I also will acknowledge before my Father who is in heaven; [33] but whoever denies me before men, I also will deny before my Father who is in heaven."

It is enough for the disciple to be like his teacher. (Matthew 10:25)

Jesus' call to his disciples was (and continues to be) a call, first and foremost, to become like him. When he called Andrew and Simon Peter, he told them that he would make them into fishers of people (Matthew 4:19). By following him, they would be transformed into his likeness. Jesus' heart would become theirs; like their master, they would long for the day when all people would hear the good news and accept the gospel message.

Jesus also warned his disciples that sharing in the life of the master is not without its challenges and difficulties: "If they have called the master of the house Beelzebul, how much more will they malign those of his household" (Matthew 10:25). At the same time, Jesus repeatedly told them not to be afraid of what might happen to them (10:26,28,31). With the confidence of one who himself had been maligned, hated, threatened, and ultimately plotted against, Jesus knew what it was to face frightening situations and triumph over them.

Because we are members of Jesus' body, we all share in his victory over the evil one. This does not mean that we will be completely free from the devil's temptations; they remain a part of all disciples' lives in this world. What it does mean is that we need never succumb, however fierce the attack may seem or however weak we may feel. Our master—the Lord Jesus Christ—is in us to comfort and strengthen us. He is our wisdom and will give us all we need as we turn to him in humble faith (Matthew 10:19-20).

In these days as we see belief in God and obedience to his commands coming under increasing fire, we can have hope and continue along the path of discipleship. Christ is in us; his love surrounds us; he will never abandon us. He will acknowledge us before the Father as we remain faithful to him. Let us not lose heart, for he who is in us is greater that he who is in the world (1 John 4:4).

"Lord Jesus, help us to trust in your presence within us. We want to become like you and be true disciples of our gracious and loving master."

Matthew 10:34–11:1

34 "Do not think that I have come to bring peace on earth; I have not come to bring peace, but a sword. 35 For I have come to set a man against his father, and a daughter against her mother, and a daughter-in-law against her mother-in-law; 36 and a man's foes will be those of his own household. 37 He who loves father or mother more than me is not worthy of me; and he who loves son or daughter more than me is not worthy of me; 38 and he who does not take his cross and follow me is not worthy of me. 39 He who finds his life will lose it, and he who loses his life for my sake will find it.
40 "He who receives you receives me, and he who receives me receives him who sent me. 41 He who receives a prophet because he is a prophet shall receive a prophet's reward, and he who receives a righteous man because he is a righteous man shall receive a righteous man's reward. 42 And whoever gives to one of these little ones even a cup of cold water because he is a disciple, truly, I say to you, he shall not lose his reward."

1 And when Jesus had finished instructing his twelve disciples, he went on from there to teach and preach in their cities. ▨▨▨

The disciple of Christ is called to witness to the new life in Christ—to testify, both by word and example, that Jesus has overcome sin and inaugurated the kingdom of God. As he explained this calling, Jesus also warned his disciples that the new life they were to manifest was radically different from life apart from God. The division Jesus spoke of occurs as the light in us becomes brighter, and the darkness around us and within us is more fully exposed.

If we want the light of Christ to shine, the darkness must give way—and this can sometimes be painful. Nevertheless, it is the calling of a disciple to maintain his or her allegiance to the Lord, and to let Christ's word, like a two-edged sword, separate darkness from light. At the same time, Jesus never leaves his disciples without the consolation of his love. They are comforted by knowing that as they share in his cross, they also share in his resurrection—both now and at the end of the ages.

Dietrich Bonhoeffer, a German Lutheran pastor who was imprisoned and put to death by the Nazi regime in Germany because he opposed its policies, put it this way:

> The final decision must be made while we are still on earth. The peace of Jesus is the cross. But the cross is the sword God wields on earth. It creates division. The son against the father, the daughter against the mother, the member of the house against the head—all this will happen in the name of God's kingdom and his peace. That is the work which Christ performs on earth.
>
> God's love is altogether different from the love of men for their own flesh and blood. God's love for man means the cross and the way of discipleship. But that cross and that way are both life and resurrection. "He that loses his life for my sake will find it." In this promise we hear the voice of him who holds the keys to death, the Son of God, who goes to the cross and the resurrection, and with him takes his own. (*The Cost of Discipleship*, 25)

Growing Tension

MATTHEW
11–12

Matthew 11:2-15

2   Now when John heard in prison about the deeds of the Christ, he sent word by his disciples 3 and said to him, "Are you he who is to come, or shall we look for another?" 4 And Jesus answered them, "Go and tell John what you hear and see: 5 the blind receive their sight and the lame walk, lepers are cleansed and the deaf hear, and the dead are raised up, and the poor have good news preached to them. 6 And blessed is he who takes no offense at me."

7   As they went away, Jesus began to speak to the crowds concerning John: "What did you go out into the wilderness to behold? A reed shaken by the wind? 8 Why then did you go out? To see a man clothed in soft raiment? Behold, those who wear soft raiment are in kings' houses. 9 Why then did you go out? To see a prophet? Yes, I tell you, and more than a prophet. 10 This is he of whom it is written, 'Behold, I send my messenger before thy face, who shall prepare thy way before thee.' 11 Truly, I say to you, among those born of women there has risen no one greater than John the Baptist; yet he who is least in the kingdom of heaven is greater than he. 12 From the days of John the Baptist until now the kingdom of heaven has suffered violence, and men of violence take it by force. 13 For all the prophets and the law prophesied until John; 14 and if you are willing to accept it, he is Elijah who is to come. 15 He who has ears to hear, let him hear."

You may have seen examples of time-lapse photography that show dramatically what happens when arid wasteland or desert is provided with a steady supply of water. Seeds spring quickly to life, and an abundant crop of flowers, vegetables, or grains demonstrates a radical change in the environment. That was the transformation Isaiah described when he spoke of the time of the Messiah (Isaiah 35:1-6). As barren land was made fruitful, useless limbs would become strong, and sightless eyes would see the glory of the Lord.

Jesus was alluding to passages such as these when he told the emissaries of John the Baptist to return to John and report the signs and wonders that were happening. His answer was not an outright claim to messiahship, but rather a reference to the phenomena that the prophets had foretold would accompany the coming of the Messiah. More significantly, Jesus' answer revealed the type of messiahship he was bringing. It was not to be an era of wrathful judgment or politico-military power, but a messiahship of healing and blessings.

The question John's disciples asked Jesus is one we must also ask: "Are you he who is to come?" (Matthew 11:3). As the answer becomes clearer from what we read in scripture and from the revelation God gives us, we need to commit ourselves to Jesus as John and his disciples did.

What should be our interior state during this search for the truth of Jesus? The Letter of James (5:7-10) said that we must let the word of God penetrate our lives. We must receive the life-giving water into our heart so that its "soil" will absorb the precious moisture that can bring growth and fruitfulness.

The author of James admonished Christians not to grumble against one another or judge one another, but rather to imitate the patient suffering of the prophets who spoke in the name of the Lord. We cannot do this by simply gritting our teeth and trying harder: It is only the Holy Spirit who will reveal to us that Jesus is the one who is to come (John 14:26). "Establish your hearts, for the coming of the Lord is at hand" (James 5:8). With expectant faith, let us ask the Holy Spirit to reveal Jesus to us.

Matthew 11:16-19

16 "But to what shall I compare this generation? It is like children sitting in the market places and calling to their playmates, 17 'We piped to you, and you did not dance; we wailed, and you did not mourn.' 18 For John came neither eating nor drinking, and they say, 'He has a demon'; 19 the Son of man came eating and drinking, and they say, 'Behold, a glutton and a drunkard, a friend of tax collectors and sinners!' Yet wisdom is justified by her deeds."

One can almost detect a note of patient weariness in the Lord's voice as he chided the crowd for its refusal to accept the truth, no matter who brought it or how it was announced. The unbelievers were like obstinate children, rejecting anything that was offered to them. How reminiscent it is of a parent coaxing youngsters to eat their greens!

Would that the consequences were less grim, the stakes less high! Both John the Baptist and Jesus came to the Jews announcing what they (as a people) had been longing to hear for centuries—the arrival of the Messiah, the Son of David, the King of Israel! Like sullen children, some of the Jews disdained John the Baptist and his message and alleged that he was possessed. When Jesus came—the one who came after John and was greater than John—they rejected him as well, charging that he was a dissolute visionary who chose to associate with unsavory people.

How many times have we heard people reject the Christian message for petty or irrational reasons? "I've got my own church in my heart; I don't need someone telling me what to do. If God is all love, how could he condemn anyone to hell?" We've all heard the rationalizations; on occasion, we may have used some of them ourselves in situations when it was inconvenient to be true to the gospel.

Matthew noted that history would be the judge of who is right and who is wrong: "Wisdom is justified by her deeds" (Matthew 11:19). The words of the psalmist are as true today as they were in the time of Jesus' earthly ministry: "The wicked will not stand in the judgment" (Psalm 1:5).

God is faithful; he will never abandon those who remain faithful to him. In Jesus, we have a loving intercessor at the right hand of the Father, constantly interceding for those who call upon his name. Let us allow the grace and love God pours out on us to work in our lives so we can experience joy and attain the promise of membership in God's own family. If we follow Jesus, we will have "the light of life" (John 8:12).

Matthew 11:20-24

²⁰ Then he began to upbraid the cities where most of his mighty works had been done, because they did not repent. ²¹ "Woe to you, Chorazin! woe to you, Bethsaida! for if the mighty works done in you had been done in Tyre and Sidon, they would have repented long ago in sackcloth and ashes. ²² But I tell you, it shall be more tolerable on the day of judgment for Tyre and Sidon than for you. ²³ And you, Capernaum, will you be exalted to heaven? You shall be brought down to Hades. For if the mighty works done in you had been done in Sodom, it would have remained until this day. ²⁴ But I tell you that it shall be more tolerable on the day of judgment for the land of Sodom than for you."

Much of Jesus' ministry in Galilee was conducted in Bethsaida, Chorazin, and especially Capernaum. There Jesus performed many healings and miracles; he opened the scriptures to the people; he told them of God's love. They heard and saw more than many other people in the Holy Land. Yet they rejected Jesus, even after God's mercy had been revealed to them. Because they refused to repent, Jesus denounced these towns.

God's mercy toward humanity is expressed through Jesus, who is one with the Father. Jesus is the center of our lives and of all our activity. He is also the object of his Father's love, through whom and in whom all things exist (Colossians 1:15-20). God sent Jesus to be our Lord and our brother, our Savior and our friend. He intends for us to walk with Jesus and to be led by him. Why, then, do we find it difficult at times to know his presence? It stems from our tendency to resist Jesus, to marginalize him, to not comprehend his centrality in God's plan of salvation. Frequently we fail to perceive his presence in our midst as he acts to guide and protect us. Sometimes we even suspect that he has abandoned us—that he has no interest in our problems and our sorrows.

Jesus, who became man for our sake is, and must be, central to our lives and to our hope for salvation. He is the source of all wisdom, power, love, and faith; he is the way to the Father; he is the brother through whom we become sons and daughters of his heavenly Father. Christ is with us—and in us—always. He promised, "I will not leave you desolate" (John 14:18). It is not Jesus who abandons us—quite the contrary. Let us examine our daily decisions to see how they reflect a reluctance to give Jesus the central place in our hearts.

We can change. If we ask in prayer, the Holy Spirit will show us who Jesus is in the Father's plan of salvation. We can read the scriptures that reveal Jesus as the Lord over all things (read Ephesians 1:3-10,17-23; Philippians 2:5-11; Colossians 1:15-20; Revelation 1:5-8). These truths can melt our hearts and fill us with a deeper desire to be united with our loving savior.

"Holy Spirit, you want to guide us into all truth. Show us Jesus, God's beloved Son. Teach us to repent for our resistance to the reality of who he is, and fill us with his love."

Matthew 11:25-27

²⁵ At that time Jesus declared, "I thank you, Father, Lord of heaven and earth, that you have hidden these things from the wise and understanding and revealed them to babes; ²⁶ yea, Father, for such was your gracious will. ²⁷ All things have been delivered to me by my Father; and no one knows the Son except the Father, and no one knows the Father except the Son and any one to whom the Son chooses to reveal him."

The Pharisees were the moral and religious pace-setters of Jesus' day. They possessed many admirable qualities, exercising great discipline in adhering to the law. The common people looked to them as models of orthodoxy. Certainly they seemed much closer to Moses than either the Sadducees or the followers of Herod. Perhaps that is why Jesus tried so hard to reach them.

The Pharisees' very position of prominence in Jewish society closed many of them off to Jesus. Something in their temperament predisposed them to reject his teaching. They were self-assured in their knowledge of God, certain that their way was right and everyone else's wrong. They lacked the very qualities that Jesus said were necessary to enter into God's kingdom: A humble child-like spirit, a sense of need, and a dependence on God rather than on self.

Jesus praised his Father for revealing the "hidden things" of salvation to those who were like "babes" (Matthew 11:25). The "wise and understanding" dismissed both his miracles and his message. The gospel writer contrasted the Lord's statement about those who rejected Jesus with words praising the "babes" who accepted Jesus as the Father's word. He then presented Christ's great invitation to come to him (11:28). The sequence highlights an important theme of Matthew's gospel: "Unless you turn and become like children, you will never enter the kingdom of heaven" (18:3).

The Pharisees had no monopoly on self-righteous thinking: We all tend to indulge in it ourselves. To stay in step with God's Spirit, however, we must constantly try to nurture a teachable spirit within ourselves. The words of Jesus call us to examine the ways in which we shut off God's revelation. Are we closed to the Spirit's voice in scripture, or in the authentic teaching of the church? Our minds can so easily adopt patterns of thinking and acting which, on the surface, seem acceptable but in truth are incompatible with God's word.

If we open our hearts, the Father can reveal to us the things that keep us from being his children. Are we willing to ask the Lord to reveal our state? We must want to become teachable in spirit; we must want to obey God because we trust him as a child trusts a parent. Then our spirits will cry out with Jesus: "I thank you, Father, Lord of heaven and earth" (Matthew 11:25).

Matthew 11:28-30

[28] "Come to me, all who labor and are heavy laden, and I will give you rest. [29] Take my yoke upon you, and learn from me; for I am gentle and lowly in heart, and you will find rest for your souls. [30] For my yoke is easy, and my burden is light."

Rejected by his own people, Jesus extended this great invitation to all persons of every nation, race, and generation. He wants all people to come to him and learn from him how to live. He wants to give a vision that will enable us to love heaven and set our sights on it, like pilgrims on a journey.

On this journey, we are often wearied by the cares and trials that face us; life can seem burdensome and oppressive. Sometimes this sense is caused by choices we have made or steps we have taken that lead us away from God. At other times, we are faced with illnesses and troubles we did not and would not bring on ourselves. Whatever the case, Jesus invites us to yoke ourselves to him and to learn from him. Then we will find rest.

Once we take this decisive step, we will experience the peace that comes only from the Prince of Peace. United with Jesus, we will be ready to learn from him. If our burden is caused by our own sin, he will teach us how to choose a new way. If it is caused by something beyond our control or power, he will teach us to hope in the reality of a place where there will be no more tears or sorrow. Just as Jesus yielded his life and will to the Father and was united with him, when we are one with Jesus we will know the unity and the peace that come from him alone.

When we decide to give up our own ways and learn from Jesus, even though we still have burdens, we will be refreshed; we will receive life. The life we receive often includes healing and deliverance that are signs of the final fullness of salvation. Seeing our lives through the prism of God's love rouses in us the desire to be united with him—to be conformed to him. Jesus' yoke *is* light because Jesus is helping us to bear the burden.

"Lord, you are sovereign over all the universe, yet you are meek and humble of heart. You have sent your own Spirit to live in us, and you want to reveal the Father to us. Protect us, Jesus, from the confusion that results when we seek answers for our lives apart from you. Shield us from the domain of self rule. Instead, establish us under your governance where you have beckoned us to come. Yes, let us be yoked to you."

Matthew 12:1-8

[1] At that time Jesus went through the grainfields on the sabbath; his disciples were hungry, and they began to pluck heads of grain and to eat. [2] But when the Pharisees saw it, they said to him, "Look, your disciples are doing what is not lawful to do on the sabbath." [3] He said to them, "Have you not read what David did, when he was hungry, and those who were with him: [4] how he entered the house of God and ate the bread of the Presence, which it was not lawful for him to eat nor for those who were with him, but only for the priests? [5] Or have you not read in the law how on the sabbath the priests in the temple profane the sabbath, and are guiltless? [6] I tell you, something greater than the temple is here. [7] And if you had known what this means, 'I desire mercy, and not sacrifice,' you would not have condemned the guiltless. [8] For the Son of man is lord of the sabbath."

I desire mercy, and not sacrifice. (Matthew 12:7)

By quoting this passage from the Old Testament (Hosea 6:6), Jesus was showing the difference between external and internal realities. The sacrifice he was disapproving was the Pharisees' belief that surface compliance to the law would make them pleasing to God. The Law of Moses required numerous rites such as ritual bathing and sacrificial offerings, all of which were supposed to make people just before God, and forbade such actions as working or making extended trips on the Sabbath.

Mercy, on the other hand, was an internal reality, requiring a new attitude of mind and heart. The Greek word for mercy used in this passage is *eleos*, a word that connotes compassion—looking kindly upon the sufferings of others. Certainly this meaning was demonstrated most perfectly in Jesus himself. Looking upon us in the misery of our separation from God, seeing our sin and its effects, Jesus showed the greatest possible mercy by becoming one like us, taking on our sins and dying, so that we might be forgiven and receive the gift of eternal life.

One can offer sacrifice repeatedly and still experience no change of heart. External actions don't necessarily produce or reflect internal transformation, even though that is often their intended purpose. When we allow the Spirit to change our hearts; when we turn away from selfish desires and seek fulfillment in the love of God; then our external actions will be signs of an interior love of God and an inclination toward him. We will have merciful hearts.

This inner mercy that Jesus wants to give us comes only through his cross, as the Holy Spirit reveals to us Jesus' selfless love. When we realize that his sacrifice is greater than anything offered in the temple under the old covenant (see Matthew 12:6, Hebrews 10:11-14), we will want to show this same mercy to others. We may continue to do the things we did before, but we do so now with a humble heart that seeks to serve God, and that brings true meaning to our actions.

"Lord Jesus, change our heart. Help us to cherish the mercy you have shown us and guard us from offering sacrifices which are but superficial actions. Father, by your Spirit, enable us to serve you and your people with love and humility."

Matthew 12:9-13

⁹ And he went on from there, and entered their synagogue. ¹⁰ And behold, there was a man with a withered hand. And they asked him, "Is it lawful to heal on the sabbath?" so that they might accuse him. ¹¹ He said to them, "What man of you, if he has one sheep and it falls into a pit on the sabbath, will not lay hold of it and lift it out? ¹² Of how much more value is a man than a sheep! So it is lawful to do good on the sabbath." ¹³ Then he said to the man, "Stretch out your hand." And the man stretched it out, and it was restored, whole like the other.

Most of the Pharisees were committed people trying to lead righteous lives before God. But their outward acts did not necessarily reflect transformed hearts or lead to an inner openness to God. Jesus often admonished them for this very thing, calling them "blind guides," "hypocrites," and "whitewashed tombs" (Matthew 23:24,25,27) who loved to justify themselves in the sight of others (Luke 16:15). Their hearts were not transformed, and thus their acts of piety served only to glorify themselves and not God.

A disciple of Christ must go beyond the righteousness of the scribes and the Pharisees which was often characterized by external pious acts (Matthew 5:20). He or she must be moved not with concern for external observances but with the motivations of the heart. Paul wrote of the condition of the human heart: "None is righteous, no, not one" (Romans 3:10). The only righteousness that is possible is that which is given to us by God through his grace, as a free and generous gift. It is the righteousness gained through the cross of Jesus and does not come from ourselves but, rather, through faith and baptism to Christ.

God wants to show us that righteousness is not something we earn by our practices but a gift freely given to us through the cross of Christ. As this truth penetrates our hearts, we begin to understand that on our own, we cannot please God. Our self-sufficient lives must be put aside in favor of a childlike trust and reliance on our loving Father. Establishing such a relationship with God fulfills the desires of our heart and helps us to joyfully fulfill the obligations of the law.

Only those who have put their own wills to death in this way can truly follow Jesus. Renouncing all self-righteousness, they rejoice with Paul: "I have been crucified with Christ; it is no longer I who live, but Christ who lives in me; and the life I now live in the flesh I live by faith in the Son of God, who loved me and gave himself for me" (Galatians 2:20).

"Lord Jesus, by the power of your Spirit in us, help us to follow you. Teach us to love as you love, so that we may build your kingdom on earth."

Matthew 12:14-21

14   But the Pharisees went out and took counsel against him, how to destroy him.

15   Jesus, aware of this, withdrew from there. And many followed him, and he healed them all, 16 and ordered them not to make him known. 17 This was to fulfil what was spoken by the prophet Isaiah: 18 "Behold, my servant whom I have chosen, my beloved with whom my soul is well pleased. I will put my Spirit upon him, and he shall proclaim justice to the Gentiles. 19 He will not wrangle or cry aloud, nor will any one hear his voice in the streets; 20 he will not break a bruised reed or quench a smoldering wick, till he brings justice to victory; 21 and in his name will the Gentiles hope."

It was inevitable that the Pharisees would eventually begin to plot against Jesus seeking to find a way to destroy him. Knowing this, Jesus withdrew from their presence, rather than confront them at that time; his hour had not yet come. This is one of the reasons why oftentimes he did not want his healings to be publicized—because the people might rally around him at the wrong time and for the wrong reasons.

In 12:18-21, Matthew cites one of the Servant of the Lord passages from Isaiah (42:1-4), suggesting the type of Messiah Jesus was to be. The Spirit of God would rest upon him and he would proclaim justice to the Gentiles. He would not make a name for himself in a way that would bring worldly attention to himself; he would harm no one, not even the weakest (bruised reed). He would be victorious in judgment, and the Gentiles would find hope in his name.

These traits stand in sharp contrast to the conception that the Jews of Jesus' time had heard about what the Messiah would be like. Despite messianic prophecies to the contrary, which were available to them in scripture, most Jews were looking for a triumphant, political Messiah through whom God would intervene to fulfill the hope of a Jewish empire.

That is why Jesus had to be restrained when he referred to himself in messianic terms. The messianic future, in the eyes of most Jews, revolved around the restoration of the kingdom of Israel, even though there was little agreement as to how this was to be accomplished. In later Judaism, there arose the expectation of two Messiahs; a Davidic, royal Messiah, and a priestly Messiah of the order of Aaron or Levi. Consider how perfectly Jesus, the son of David (Matthew 1:1) and eternal high priest (Hebrews 7:22–8:6), fulfilled both expectations when he established his kingdom—the Israel of God.

"Lord Jesus, we believe in you and worship you as the Messiah, promised in the Old Testament and revealed in the New. Increase our understanding of what it means that you became man and died for us. Help us to change our lives in response to your love and sacrifice so that even now, we may begin to live in the eternal kingdom of the Father."

Matthew 12:22-37

²² Then a blind and dumb demoniac was brought to him, and he healed him, so that the dumb man spoke and saw. ²³ And all the people were amazed, and said, "Can this be the Son of David?" ²⁴ But when the Pharisees heard it they said, "It is only by Beelzebul, the prince of demons, that this man casts out demons." ²⁵ Knowing their thoughts, he said to them, "Every kingdom divided against itself is laid waste, and no city or house divided against itself will stand; ²⁶ and if Satan casts out Satan, he is divided against himself; how then will his kingdom stand? ²⁷ And if I cast out demons by Beelzebul, by whom do your sons cast them out? Therefore they shall be your judges. ²⁸ But if it is by the Spirit of God that I cast out demons, then the kingdom of God has come upon you. ²⁹ Or how can one enter a strong man's house and plunder his goods, unless he first binds the strong man? Then indeed he may plunder his house. ³⁰ He who is not with me is against me, and he who does not gather with me scatters. ³¹ Therefore I tell you, every sin and blasphemy will be forgiven men, but the blasphemy against the Spirit will not be forgiven. ³² And whoever says a word against the Son of man will be forgiven; but whoever speaks against the Holy Spirit will not be forgiven, either in this age or in the age to come. ³³ "Either make the tree good, and its fruit good; or make the tree bad, and its fruit bad; for the tree is known by its fruit. ³⁴ You brood of vipers! how can you speak good, when you are evil? For out of the abundance of the heart the mouth speaks. ³⁵ The good man out of his good treasure brings forth good, and the evil man out of his evil treasure brings forth evil. ³⁶ I tell you, on the day of judgment men will render account for every careless word they utter; ³⁷ for by your words you will be justified, and by your words you will be condemned."

Matthew's gospel gradually reveals more and more about who Jesus was *and* who he was not. On one such occasion, Jesus faced a serious charge from scribes who asserted that he was possessed by "Beelzebul" (a demonic title meaning "lord of the flies"). They accused him of exorcising demons "by the prince of demons" (Matthew 12:24).

Jesus exposed the fallacy of their indictment with a common sense question: "If Satan casts out Satan, he is divided against himself; how then will his kingdom stand?" (Matthew 12:26). Out of jealousy and self-righteousness, the scribes had become blind to the obvious: By casting out demons and healing people, Jesus was *destroying* Satan's kingdom, not *building* it.

In contrast, Jesus implicitly suggested that he had come to establish the kingdom of God by first plundering the house of "the strong man" (Matthew 12:29). To his detractors who made such charges, Jesus solemnly warned: "Whoever speaks against the Holy Spirit will not be forgiven" (12:32). The context here is significant. Jesus was addressing leaders who attributed the saving work of God to Satan. They twisted the truth, refusing God's gift of salvation and placing others at risk as well.

The first part of Jesus' statement proclaimed that God was willing to forgive people all other sins and blasphemies. It marked yet another step in the progressive revelation of the son of man: He has the power to forgive.

Matthew combined this rejection story with a series of skeptical responses. The sequence provides a cumulative effect. Jesus' identity emerges more clearly because he refuted the negative caricatures painted by his opponents. At the same time, Matthew provided a striking contradiction: The scribes and religious authorities—whom we would expect to welcome Jesus—rejected him. The disciples and the crowds of simple, poor people—perhaps because of their neediness, but certainly because of their openness—saw Jesus as the Messiah inaugurating the reign of God in power.

"Lord Jesus, like some of those who met you, we are often troubled by doubts, fears, and prejudices. When your Spirit touches us, however, we know that you are our Lord and Savior. Help us to come to know you more deeply, so that we may yield our lives to you completely."

Matthew 12:38-42

[38] Then some of the scribes and Pharisees said to him, "Teacher, we wish to see a sign from you." [39] But he answered them, "An evil and adulterous generation seeks for a sign; but no sign shall be given to it except the sign of the prophet Jonah. [40] For as Jonah was three days and three nights in the belly of the whale, so will the Son of man be three days and three nights in the heart of the earth. [41] The men of Nineveh will arise at the judgment with this generation and condemn it; for they repented at the preaching of Jonah, and behold, something greater than Jonah is here. [42] The queen of the South will arise at the judgment with this generation and condemn it; for she came from the ends of the earth to hear the wisdom of Solomon, and behold, something greater than Solomon is here."

The Jews of the New Testament times expected that the messianic age would be ushered in with spectacular signs and miracles. They were looking for a Messiah who would lead the nation in triumph over the Gentiles. These "signs and wonders" would reveal and confirm the intervention of God on behalf of his people.

During his ministry in Galilee (Matthew 8–10), Jesus performed many signs, such as healing a leper and raising a dead girl to life. Even so, the scribes and Pharisees still came to Jesus demanding signs to attest to his authenticity (12:38).

Jesus rebuked them for their unbelief. He contended that if the Ninevites (a people hated for their savagery and ungodliness—see Nahum 1:1–3:19) had repented at the preaching of Jonah, and if the Queen of Sheba had traveled great distances to hear the wisdom of Solomon (and now there was one even greater), should not God's people respond to the teacher in their midst? There would be but one sign for them—the "sign of Jonah"; Jesus himself would spend three days in the bowels of the earth before rising to life in victory over death. The ultimate sign would be the crucified Jesus rising out of the tomb, bearing witness to the Father's love.

Like people of every age, we look for signs of God's presence and activity. Often, the sign we seek is not the one Jesus has given: The sign of his cross, the sign of love. In every generation, God calls people to himself and transforms them by the work of the cross. "We were buried therefore with him by baptism into death, so that as Christ was raised from the dead by the glory of the Father, we too might walk in newness of life . . . . We know that our old self was crucified with him so that the sinful body might be destroyed, and we might no longer be enslaved to sin" (Romans 6:4,6). The cross of Christ, whose power transforms lives, is the sign Christ gives.

"Lord Jesus, we believe that in your infinite power, no sign is beyond you. Yet in your love, you leave us with the sign of your victory—the cross. May your Holy Spirit show us that your cross is the only sign we need. Let that sign touch our lives and change us."

Matthew 12:43-45

43 "When the unclean spirit has gone out of a man, he passes through waterless places seeking rest, but he finds none. 44 Then he says, 'I will return to my house from which I came.' And when he comes he finds it empty, swept, and put in order. 45 Then he goes and brings with him seven other spirits more evil than himself, and they enter and dwell there; and the last state of that man becomes worse than the first. So shall it be also with this evil generation."

When the unclean spirit that had been expelled from the man returned to his "house" where he had formerly taken up residence, it was "empty, swept and put in order" (Matthew 12:44). The unclean spirit may have left the man temporarily, but nothing good had replaced it. There had been no fundamental change in the person, and so it was possible for seven additional spirits, who were even more evil, to dwell there.

Jesus concluded: "So shall it be also with this evil generation" (Matthew 12:45). Presumably, he was referring to those who opposed him during his time on earth, including some of the leading Pharisees. They had witnessed Jesus' miracles continually—the expelling of demons, many healings, the multiplication of food. Yet these signs did not change their hearts. They went on living as they had before, without the life-changing transformation that was needed for them to become disciples of Christ.

These people "missed the boat," so to speak. They had the chance to drink the "living water" (John 4:10) and they declined. This hardened their hearts still further, until they were totally blinded to the love that God was holding out to them through Jesus. Their hearts were empty of love, and this emptiness—like a vacuum—allowed sin to rush in.

If we want to be Jesus' disciples, we cannot simply chase evil out of our lives. We must replace sin with goodness, with the very life of Christ. We are not passive observers in this spiritual battle. We can take positive steps to fill ourselves with Christ, through the sacraments and prayer, through fellowship with other committed Christians, and through meditation on the word of God.

"Put on the whole armor of God, that you may be able to stand against the wiles of the devil," Paul advised in his letter to the Ephesians (6:11). This armor included the breastplate of righteousness, the shield of faith, the helmet of salvation, and the sword of the Spirit, "which is the word of God" (6:17). Thus equipped, we can persevere, with God's grace, to obtain the victory.

"Holy Spirit, help us to equip ourselves to do battle with sin in our lives. Help us to guard our thoughts and our hearts. Arm us with righteousness, faith, and your word, so that we can 'fight the good fight of the faith' " (1 Timothy 6:12).

Matthew 12:46-50

⁴⁶ While he was still speaking to the people, behold, his mother and his brethren stood outside, asking to speak to him. ⁴⁸ But he replied to the man who told him, "Who is my mother, and who are my brethren?" ⁴⁹ And stretching out his hand toward his disciples, he said, "Here are my mother and my brethren! ⁵⁰ For whoever does the will of my Father in heaven is my brother, and sister, and mother."

"Who is my mother, and who are my brethren?" (Matthew 12:48)

Do you know who you are? Evolutionists tell us we are biological beings that can be traced back to the apes. Economists see us as consumer statistics, while demographers see us as population statistics. Scripture, however, says we belong to God.

Where does *your* identity come from? We introduce ourselves by using our names, which reflect the family into which we were born or have married. Jesus authorized his disciples to claim a new identification. Those who follow Christ become part of his spiritual family, membership given through faith and baptism. Most of us were probably baptized as infants, yet we can ratify or reject our membership in Christ's family.

The intent of Jesus' often misunderstood teaching is not to disown blood relatives, but to honor those who have answered God's call to membership in a new community—the church. Through this blessing, God views us as his children—brothers and sisters to his Son. Through obedience to God and his word, we affirm our membership in his family, which was initiated at baptism when the seed of faith was planted in us. What a wonderful privilege it is that God would consider mere mortals as part of the lineage of his Son, Jesus!

At first glance, this incident with Jesus' family members seems to be almost a rebuke to his blood relations. In fact, it is a compliment, the expression of Jesus' gratitude to his mother, Mary. More than anyone else, Mary was the perfect example of obedience to the Father's will. "Behold, I am the handmaid of the Lord; let it be to me according to your word" (Luke 1:38). Mary's heartfelt response demonstrated a surrendering of her own will so that God's eternal plan for salvation could be fulfilled. She saw herself in a proper perspective—submitted to God and his plan. Mary's "yes" to God was one of many instances in her lifetime when she would embrace the will of God. She is, par excellence, a disciple of Jesus and thus a member of his family.

"Lord Jesus, help us to make the decision every day to do the Father's will, so that we may receive the fullness of your promises. We embrace the new family to which you have joined us by our faith. We praise and thank you for this divine union."

Parables of the Kingdom

MATTHEW
13:1-52

Matthew 13:1-9

[1] That same day Jesus went out of the house and sat beside the sea. [2] And great crowds gathered about him, so that he got into a boat and sat there; and the whole crowd stood on the beach. [3] And he told them many things in parables, saying: "A sower went out to sow. [4] And as he sowed, some seeds fell along the path, and the birds came and devoured them. [5] Other seeds fell on rocky ground, where they had not much soil, and immediately they sprang up, since they had no depth of soil, [6] but when the sun rose they were scorched; and since they had no root they withered away. [7] Other seeds fell upon thorns, and the thorns grew up and choked them. [8] Other seeds fell on good soil and brought forth grain, some a hundredfold, some sixty, some thirty. [9] He who has ears, let him hear."

Jesus described four possible responses to the word of God. The seed on the footpath refers to those people who quickly lose the word because they do not understand it. The seed on rocky ground describes those who have no firm foundation. The seed fallen among thorns relates to those who receive the good news, but later abandon it for the lure of the world. Finally, the seed on good soil describes those who hear the word of God, accept it, and conform their lives to it.

Most of us would like to identify ourselves with the seed planted in good soil. If we examine ourselves closely, however, we would probably see how some other part of the story might be just as applicable. God's call to us often involves more than we think.

It is a call to nothing less that total dedication, to living so that we give glory to God.

Every day, God asks us to decide whether or not we will live for his glory. When Jesus came upon the man who had been born blind, he said that this had happened so that God could be glorified in his works (John 9:3-4). When he was healed, the man joyfully proclaimed what God had done. Despite pressure and threats from the Pharisees, he continued to glorify God. We all face a similar choice: We can give glory to God for his work in us, or we can allow fear and outside pressure to overcome us. We can fearlessly proclaim the marvels of God, or we can be bound by fears of rejection to the point where we dilute God's action and deny him glory.

Do we believe that the gospel has changed us, or do we believe change happened as the result of our own efforts? Do we believe that everyone needs salvation, or that Jesus is just an option in God's plan? The answers to these questions can be found by examining the fruit that is being borne in our lives.

God is asking us if we want to be vibrant Christians who transform the world or simply agreeable people who sometimes pray and occasionally read scripture. If we acknowledge the action of God in our lives and desire to serve him, the seed will be productive. We will yield thirty, sixty, or even a hundred-fold.

Matthew 13:10-17

[10] Then the disciples came and said to him, "Why do you speak to them in parables?" [11] And he answered them, "To you it has been given to know the secrets of the kingdom of heaven, but to them it has not been given. [12] For to him who has will more be given, and he will have abundance; but from him who has not, even what he has will be taken away. [13] This is why I speak to them in parables, because seeing they do not see, and hearing they do not hear, nor do they understand. [14] With them indeed is fulfilled the prophecy of Isaiah which says: 'You shall indeed hear but never understand, and you shall indeed see but never perceive. [15] For this people's heart has grown dull, and their ears are heavy of hearing, and their eyes they have closed, lest they should perceive with their eyes, and hear with their ears, and understand with their heart, and turn for me to heal them.' [16] But blessed are your eyes, for they see, and your ears, for they hear. [17] Truly, I say to you, many prophets and righteous men longed to see what you see, and did not see it, and to hear what you hear, and did not hear it."

To you it has been given to know the secrets of the kingdom of heaven, but to them it has not been given. (Matthew 13:11)

Does God only reveal himself to a few select people? Did Jesus intentionally exclude some of his listeners from understanding and accepting his message? These provocative questions call for answers.

Parables are stories that employ everyday situations to deliver a message or make a point. They are not necessarily real life stories, but rather help to give memorable expression to teachings. Jesus' parables caused people to reflect on his message and to accept it or reject it. Many of the Jews of Jesus' time responded to him with hostility. Jesus referred to them as the ones who would hear, but not understand (Matthew 13:13). His aim in using parables was not to keep the truth hidden, but to convey spiritual truths in a way that would elicit a reaction.

Our understanding of this passage rests on the truth of who God is in and of himself. He is complete and perfect in all his ways; his purpose in creating us was that we should share life with him forever. It is wrong to say that God gives his truth to some and withholds it from others. His love and his desire are the same for all; he wants all people to come to know him. The difference is in the response. "Hearing" or "seeing" connotes a spiritual understanding or perception of the truth. It is not a question of God's refusal to give, but of our refusal to accept.

To those whose hearts are open to receive, God's word brings truth and life. The disposition of the hearer's heart is what matters. Those who didn't understand Jesus' parables were those whose hearts had grown dull, who had closed their eyes. An "open" heart means *actively* choosing to take hold of his words and applying them in our lives.

Let us examine the disposition of our hearts. Are they open to God's word and unencumbered by competing thoughts, desires, fears, and judgments? Are we actively seeking to "see" and "hear" his truth? Jesus promised us: "Ask, and it will be given you; seek, and you will find, knock, and it will be opened to you" (Matthew 7:7).

"Come, Holy Spirit, we are seeking. Reveal the truth to us as we open our hearts to receive it."

Matthew 13:18-23

[18] "Hear then the parable of the sower. [19] When any one hears the word of the kingdom and does not understand it, the evil one comes and snatches away what is sown in his heart; this is what was sown along the path. [20] As for what was sown on rocky ground, this is he who hears the word and immediately receives it with joy; [21] yet he has no root in himself, but endures for a while, and when tribulation or persecution arises on account of the word, immediately he falls away. [22] As for what was sown among thorns, this is he who hears the word, but the cares of the world and the delight in riches choke the word, and it proves unfruitful. [23] As for what was sown on good soil, this is he who hears the word and understands it; he indeed bears fruit, and yields, in one case a hundredfold, in another sixty, and in another thirty."

The parable of the sower and the seed (Matthew 13:4-9; 18-23) reflects everyday farming practices in Palestine during Jesus' time. The images it evokes would have been easily understood by those listening to Jesus. In the parable, the soil represents the various degrees of openness in those who heard the gospel message.

Jesus described the responses that different people make in their walk of faith toward maturity. First is the hearer of the word who doesn't understand or fully accept it (Matthew 13:19). Second are those who understand but cannot stand up to the challenge of persecution or suffering (13:21). The third group hears and accepts the word but is distracted by the world (13:22). A final group of believers hears the word, understands it, and responds positively (13:23).

When we first come to faith in Jesus, we are like "babes in Christ" (1 Corinthians 3:1) who—over time—may achieve maturity. This progression, from infancy to maturity, does not happen through self-effort, but comes through the work of the Holy Spirit in us. "For God is at work in you, both to will and to work for his good pleasure" (Philippians 2:13). With our cooperation, God will bring to completion what he has started in us for he wants a plentiful harvest.

We can cooperate with God's grace in order to see fruit in our lives: God has promised us the Holy Spirit who will teach us all things (John 16:13). Christ himself, through his blood, cleanses us from our sins and dead works and makes us just before God (Hebrews 9:14; Romans 5:9). Through his cross, Jesus strengthens us in times of trial and weakness (1 Corinthians 1:18). He draws us together through baptism into one body, his church, where we drink of the one Spirit and are sustained in word and sacrament (1 Corinthians 12:13). He gives us his very body and blood as food from heaven to nourish us (1 Corinthians 11:23-26).

Jesus himself provides for us in our walk of faith. Our response determines the yield in our lives. Let us pray that we will be open to him so that we may yield a wonderfully bountiful harvest.

Matthew 13:24-30

²⁴ Another parable he put before them, saying, "The kingdom of heaven may be compared to a man who sowed good seed in his field; ²⁵ but while men were sleeping, his enemy came and sowed weeds among the wheat, and went away. ²⁶ So when the plants came up and bore grain, then the weeds appeared also. ²⁷ And the servants of the householder came and said to him, 'Sir, did you not sow good seed in your field? How then has it weeds?' ²⁸ He said to them, 'An enemy has done this.' The servants said to him, 'Then do you want us to go and gather them?' ²⁹ But he said, 'No; lest in gathering the weeds you root up the wheat along with them. ³⁰ Let both grow together until the harvest; and at harvest time I will tell the reapers, Gather the weeds first and bind them in bundles to be burned, but gather the wheat into my barn.' "

The weed referred to by Jesus in this parable is a type of darnel. It grows close to the wheat, but since its roots are deeper and stronger, any attempt to uproot it inevitably uproots the wheat as well. Thus, if eliminated prematurely, there would be no harvest at all.

The kingdom of heaven inaugurated by Jesus "may be compared to a man who sowed good seed in his field" (Matthew 13:24). Jesus, in his death and resurrection, conquered sin and death, and the work of the kingdom advanced. And yet the enemy—the weed—is still at work among us (13:28).

In faith, however, we know that God's timing is perfect. We may long for the day when evil is completely destroyed, but we know that God in his wisdom has a plan for his kingdom and the harvest. For now, it would be premature to uproot the darnel. At the end of time, however, when the new heaven and the new earth have come, every hint of sin and evil will be wiped away.

In the meantime, we must endure the evil that is in the world. Even Jesus underwent temptation by Satan (Matthew 4:1-11). The Father permits us to be tempted too, and yet our victory lies with Jesus. With the eyes of faith, we must learn to detect the weeds among the wheat. We must resist evil wherever we see it and stand up for righteousness. In this, we can depend on God's help, relying on the truth of his word, the power of his love, and his grace and strength. As the Father sent angels to minister to Jesus in the desert after his confrontation with the devil (4:11), we, too, can count on our Father to care for us.

Someday, the weeds and the wheat will be separated. The weeds will be burned, while the wheat will be gathered together (Matthew 13:30). At this final judgment, evil will be defeated, and the righteous "will shine like the sun in the kingdom of their Father" (13:43).

"Lord Jesus, you know how much we want to be part of your eternal kingdom. Protect and guide us when we encounter evil in the world. When we face temptation, send your angels to minister to us, as your Father did for you. With your Holy Spirit to guide us, we can face the battles that lie ahead."

Matthew 13:31-35

[31] Another parable he put before them, saying, "The kingdom of heaven is like a grain of mustard seed which a man took and sowed in his field; [32] it is the smallest of all seeds, but when it has grown it is the greatest of shrubs and becomes a tree, so that the birds of the air come and make nests in its branches."

[33] He told them another parable. "The kingdom of heaven is like leaven which a woman took and hid in three measures of flour, till it was all leavened."

[34] All this Jesus said to the crowds in parables; indeed he said nothing to them without a parable. [35] This was to fulfil what was spoken by the prophet: "I will open my mouth in parables, I will utter what has been hidden since the foundation of the world."

Jesus chose his parables carefully. He wanted the jostling masses to understand an essential point about the kingdom of God: *It is for everyone*, not just the Pharisees or the Sanhedrin, the elect or politically powerful. God's kingdom on earth, which Jesus inaugurated, is intended for every person ever born. No one is too small, or inconsequential, or insignificant to be welcomed into it.

It was not by accident that Matthew placed these parables at the center of his gospel. The apex of the gospel, the truth revealed by Jesus, rests on this—that the kingdom of God is open to all. It was initiated in an obscure corner of the world, among a small, inconspicuous people, at a time in history in which global communications were nonexistent. This is the mystery, the wonder of

God's work among his people! What seems impossibly insignificant can have great results.

In our sometimes mundane homes or jobs, in the routine tasks of our lives, we should never underestimate what the Lord can do through us as we respond obediently to him. Most of us, at heart, think of ourselves as ordinary, and of what we do as relatively insignificant in the eternal scheme of things. And yet, to God, we are precious, every one of us, and each essential to the body of Christ. By equating significance with recognition, we fall into the trap of thinking that what we do is not terribly important.

This is not the way God thinks! Just look at how he ushered in his kingdom on earth, through a poor carpenter from a subjugated people. Or how he produced a saint from Therese of Lisieux, a simple French nun hidden away in a Carmelite convent; or how he made a beacon of his love shine forth to the world from Mother Teresa, an elderly Albanian nun. Many saints, in fact, came from simple families that trusted in the Lord. Let us persevere and allow the mustard seed and leaven in our lives to grow and become transforming.

"Lord, nothing is too small, no one too inconsequential, for you to work through. The growth of your life in us and your kingdom on earth is entirely your work. Give us the grace to realize that you are always working, even when we can't see it. Grant us the faith and the vision to believe that there is no limit to what you can do as long as we remain obedient to you."

Matthew 13:36-43

[36] Then he left the crowds and went into the house. And his disciples came to him, saying, "Explain to us the parable of the weeds of the field." [37] He answered, "He who sows the good seed is the Son of man; [38] the field is the world, and the good seed means the sons of the kingdom; the weeds are the sons of the evil one, [39] and the enemy who sowed them is the devil; the harvest is the close of the age, and the reapers are angels. [40] Just as the weeds are gathered and burned with fire, so will it be at the close of the age. [41] The Son of man will send his angels, and they will gather out of his kingdom all causes of sin and all evildoers, [42] and throw them into the furnace of fire; there men will weep and gnash their teeth. [43] Then the righteous will shine like the sun in the kingdom of their Father. He who has ears, let him hear."

Have you ever tried to weed a garden in which the plants were still seedlings? Unless you are very familiar with how your plants should look at that stage, it is easy to uproot your crops along with the weeds. Desirable plants and weeds can look much alike, especially in their early stages, and weeding can result in loss of some of the good plants.

This is the explanation of the parable of the good seed and the weeds (see Matthew 13:24-30 for the actual parable). Most commentators believe that this parable reflects the experience of the primitive church as it tried to grapple with the problem of good and evil in its midst. Our initial reaction to weeds among our wheat might be to try and eliminate all the weeds immediately.

Jesus suggested a more cautious approach. The need for prudence is made even clearer by the identification in the Greek text (13:25,36) of the weed looking deceptively like wheat.

The first believers quickly discovered that the church contained both wheat and weeds—those who lived what they professed, and those who claimed allegiance to Christ but showed no evidence of it. The desire to root out all those who showed no signs of new life had to be curbed in the light of this parable. What if their criteria for discerning wheat from weeds were faulty? Being themselves fallen men and women, how would they be able to distinguish in all circumstances between real and false spirituality?

The inclusion of this parable and its explanation in the gospel shows that the church did not see itself as the final judge; the dispensation of justice rests with God alone. The leaders of the early church saw that the time of harvest, the final judgment, was being delayed so that as many as possible could receive the mercy and salvation of Jesus and come into his kingdom (see 2 Peter 3:9). Until then, the church has to encourage, to preach, to strengthen, and to teach all who will listen in the hope that they might believe and be converted.

"Father, we know that there are both wheat and weeds in the church of your Son, Jesus Christ. Keep us from judging and condemning others. Give us instead a share in your mercy so that we will love and serve as many as we can, that they may be strengthened and renewed in faith."

Matthew 13:44-46

⁴⁴ "The kingdom of heaven is like treasure hidden in a field, which a man found and covered up; then in his joy he goes and sells all that he has and buys that field.
⁴⁵ "Again, the kingdom of heaven is like a merchant in search of fine pearls, ⁴⁶ who, on finding one pearl of great value, went and sold all that he had and bought it."

What does being a citizen of the kingdom of heaven mean to you? Take a moment to think about this question before you continue on. If we don't have a deep appreciation of what it means to be in the kingdom of God, then it is unlikely that we will consider it worth sacrificing everything in order to attain it.

If, on the other hand, we know in our hearts the deep love of Jesus and how he came to rescue us from the power of sin and condemnation by his death and resurrection, we will let nothing come between ourselves and him. He has forgiven every sin of those who have turned to him in repentance; he wants to restore us to true life with the Father. If we recall these things with gratitude each day, we will know that the kingdom of God is like a treasure or a pearl of great value and we will do all we can to obtain it.

Scripture itself provides us with many examples of people who knew the worth of the kingdom and of those who did not. Consider the case of the rich young man (see Matthew 19:16-22). Jesus tested his heart by asking him to abandon his beloved worldly possessions. This was more than the wealthy Israelite expected to be asked to do. His wealth was more meaningful to him than Jesus; his material goods were more real than the promise of eternal life.

St. Paul's outlook was the complete antithesis of this (see Philippians 3:7-9). He considered everything as loss compared to the inestimable treasure of knowing Jesus and serving him. His greatest desire was to know Christ; all else was refuse—in Greek, *skubalon*, which is literally "dung"—(Philippians 3:8).

If we are to be like Paul and treasure the kingdom of God, we need to know God's love in our hearts. The experience of God's love will make us long for his kingdom above all else. The Holy Spirit will reveal the depths of this love to us as we pray and ask the Lord to show it to us.

"Holy Spirit, come and touch our hearts that we may know the great love of God the Father in Jesus Christ and, knowing this, may come to understand that the kingdom of God is worth everything."

Matthew 13:47-52

[47] "Again, the kingdom of heaven is like a net which was thrown into the sea and gathered fish of every kind; [48] when it was full, men drew it ashore and sat down and sorted the good into vessels but threw away the bad. [49] So it will be at the close of the age. The angels will come out and separate the evil from the righteous, [50] and throw them into the furnace of fire; there men will weep and gnash their teeth.

[51] "Have you understood all this?" They said to him, "Yes."

[52] And he said to them, "Therefore every scribe who has been trained for the kingdom of heaven is like a householder who brings out of his treasure what is new and what is old."

Jesus maintained that "every scribe who had been trained for the kingdom of heaven" (Matthew 13:52) was a person of unique privilege. Such a person, taught in the way of God according to the old covenant, would come face to face with the blessing and power of God in the gospel. Through the Holy Spirit, God could build upon such a person's knowledge of the Old Testament to enrich him in the gospel of Christ, for his own benefit and for that of the whole church. Some scholars suspect that Matthew himself became such a Christian scribe, and that these words, which appear only in Matthew's gospel, are a kind of self-portrait.

There is a challenge, however, that attends this privilege—how to know what is good and what is bad? Not only are there elements of the old covenant that are more or less important under the new, the new covenant itself needs to be understood and interpreted correctly. A scribe had to recognize and deal with the prejudices that he carried in his own mind about the word of God. How was a scribe to know what to cherish and use, and what to throw away?

Paul provided some insight into this question when he wrote: "The aim of our charge is love that issues from a pure heart and a good conscience and sincere faith" (1 Timothy 1:5). Paul knew that whatever came from God would lead to love and bear true, lasting fruit among God's people. The Holy Spirit, poured out at Pentecost, would enlighten the minds and "guide . . . into all the truth" (John 16:13) those who prayerfully desire to know and obey the will of God.

The challenge to the scribe is not lost on us today. The last thirty-five years have been a time of tremendous change in the church and in the world. We need to ask the Holy Spirit, who has bestowed on us gifts of wisdom and discernment, to help us to determine which—among the many new and old things we encounter each day—are consistent with God's will and will bear fruit among his people. The question becomes not "old is good" or "new is bad" but, "What will lead us to holiness, love of God, and the building up of the church?"

Demonstrations of the Kingdom

MATTHEW
13:53–16:12

Matthew 13:53-58

[53] And when Jesus had finished these parables, he went away from there, [54] and coming to his own country he taught them in their synagogue, so that they were astonished, and said, "Where did this man get this wisdom and these mighty works? [55] Is not this the carpenter's son? Is not his mother called Mary? And are not his brethren James and Joseph and Simon and Judas? [56] And are not all his sisters with us? Where then did this man get all this?" [57] And they took offense at him. But Jesus said to them, "A prophet is not without honor except in his own country and in his own house." [58] And he did not do many mighty works there, because of their unbelief.

Routines can be helpful in our daily lives. At home, we establish routines for caring for our families, for preparing and sharing meals, for the cleaning and upkeep of our houses. At work or school, routines help us accomplish our goals more reliably and efficiently. In a healthy sense, we develop routines in our relationships with God and our Christian brothers and sisters—patterns of personal prayer, attendance at church services, Christian fellowship. It is possible in our routines, however, to become so accustomed to the commonplace (to what "usually happens") that we close ourselves off to the possibility of new and different things.

This is perhaps what happened to the townspeople of Nazareth who demonstrated an inability to rise above their ordinary, mundane impressions of Jesus. He had lived among them, spoken with them, eaten with them, worked with them. They knew his family, his parents and relatives. He had become a part of the comfortable routine of life.

But the routine was broken when Jesus demonstrated wisdom and miraculous powers among them (Matthew 13:54). So, despite their knowledge of Jesus, "they took offense at him" and found him altogether too much for them (13:57). As a result, they were unable to recognize that he was the Son of God and closed themselves to his power at work among them. Their own opinions, formed over many years, weighed more heavily in their thinking than the power they had seen at work among them. And so, Jesus "did not work many mighty works there because of their unbelief" (13:58).

Sometimes we develop similar attitudes that limit the work of God among us. We are used to a Christianity in which healings do not occur, people do not hear God speak, and we do not expect God's comfort. And so, we doubt that Jesus will heal us, speak to us, or comfort us, despite what we see in scripture or through the testimony of countless saints. Such attitudes are in opposition to faith in Jesus. Faith calls us to put aside our prejudices, preconceptions, and the like, and to look expectantly toward God. As we do this, we will see God work in power among us.

"Lord Jesus, help me to approach each day with an expectant heart, to believe that you will work among us. Help me to expect even the unexpected, that you might speak to me, comfort me, heal me. Let not my routines and beliefs stand in the way of your work among us."

Matthew 14:1-12

[1]   At that time Herod the tetrarch heard about the fame of Jesus; [2] and he said to his servants, "This is John the Baptist, he has been raised from the dead; that is why these powers are at work in him." [3] For Herod had seized John and bound him and put him in prison, for the sake of Herodias, his brother Philip's wife; [4] because John said to him, "It is not lawful for you to have her." [5] And though he wanted to put him to death, he feared the people, because they held him to be a prophet. [6] But when Herod's birthday came, the daughter of Herodias danced before the company, and pleased Herod, [7] so that he promised with an oath to give her whatever she might ask. [8] Prompted by her mother, she said, "Give me the head of John the Baptist here on a platter." [9] And the king was sorry; but because of his oaths and his guests he commanded it to be given; [10] he sent and had John beheaded in the prison, [11] and his head was brought on a platter and given to the girl, and she brought it to her mother. [12] And his disciples came and took the body and buried it; and they went and told Jesus.

John the Baptist both terrified and fascinated Herod. Although Herod had thrown John in prison, he sensed that the people were right: John was a prophet (Matthew 14:5). And so he "was sorry" (14:9) when he found that he had to fulfill his reckless oath and have John beheaded.

Yet Herod's situation was more pitiable than John's. Although he endured a tragic death, John the Baptist had done his work on earth—he had been the one to "go before the Lord to prepare his ways" (Luke 1:76). Jesus described him as greater than any born of woman (Matthew 11:11). John would enjoy eternal life with God.

Herod, on the other hand, had been given the honor of knowing one of the greatest prophets of all time. Instead of being transformed by this experience, he chose to continue in his sinful ways. Perhaps he feared what would happen to his life if he let John's message penetrate him. Surely, he would have had to change. Instead of grasping onto the truth, Herod—for all time—would be known as a man who was manipulated to do what he did not want to do: Sentence John the Baptist to death.

Fear of change can sometimes lead us to hold on to negative or sinful patterns in our lives as well. We have the honor of knowing Jesus Christ on a personal basis. That prospect can make us rejoice, but it can also make us fearful. As a committed Christian, what will the Lord call us to change in our lives? Will we have to give up habits that lead us away from him, or friendships that influence us negatively? Will we have to risk persecution by taking unpopular stands?

"We are not of those who shrink back and are destroyed, but of those who have faith and keep their souls" (Hebrews 10:39). Let us not draw back from the Lord, even when his truth challenges all the assumptions upon which we have built our lives. His truth is the door to eternal life.

"Father, give us the courage to follow you, no matter what the cost. Even if we must face the pain of change, help us to trust in your love for us and your plan for our lives."

Matthew 14:13-21

13 Now when Jesus heard this, he withdrew from there in a boat to a lonely place apart. But when the crowds heard it, they followed him on foot from the towns. 14 As he went ashore he saw a great throng; and he had compassion on them, and healed their sick. 15 When it was evening, the disciples came to him and said, "This is a lonely place, and the day is now over; send the crowds away to go into the villages and buy food for themselves." 16 Jesus said, "They need not go away; you give them something to eat." 17 They said to him, "We have only five loaves here and two fish." 18 And he said, "Bring them here to me." 19 Then he ordered the crowds to sit down on the grass; and taking the five loaves and the two fish he looked up to heaven, and blessed, and broke and gave the loaves to the disciples, and the disciples gave them to the crowds. 20 And they all ate and were satisfied. And they took up twelve baskets full of the broken pieces left over. 21 And those who ate were about five thousand men, besides women and children.

Not all at once, but little by little, the Lord calls us, even at times when we do not expect or maybe never even notice. He may begin by whispering little questions to our hearts. Or perhaps little annoyances of life will persist and pile up, until we begin to question who we are and who God is. We begin to take on an eternal perspective, even without realizing that such thoughts are the result of God moving in us, calling us to himself. Little by little, we begin to respond in ways that we never would have done before. Maybe we begin going to Mass during the week, we start reading scripture or pick up a book of spiritual reading that we saw in the back of church. Very often, this is how we begin a deeper walk with Jesus—not simply by our own design, but as a result of God's love and mercy for us.

What can separate us from the love of God? Nothing. All throughout our lives he whispers and calls—he even shouts at times—because he wants to share his life with us. God's love for us is such that he does more than just maintain and sustain our lives. He is always at work to form us into more perfect sons and daughters, filled with the power of the Holy Spirit and united as one body under Christ, our head.

Jesus demonstrated this constant work on our behalf when he miraculously fed the five thousand. The disciples suggested dismissing the crowd, but Jesus hadn't finished caring for them. His generosity and graciousness far surpass anything we can imagine, and he freely gives to anyone who comes to him. After all, what could we pay for a lifetime of overflowing grace and love—the equivalent of a few pieces of bread and some fish?

This abundance of grace is ours for the asking. When we come humbly to the Lord's table today to receive the bread of life, let us ask Jesus for everything he wants to give us. God's provision for us is boundless and immeasurable. Let nothing stand in his way today—no grudges, no anger, no bitterness, no repeating sin pattern. Let us turn to God and allow his grace to heal us and make us what he has called us to become—sons and daughters who reflect his love in all they do and say.

Matthew 14:22-36

22   Then he made the disciples get into the boat and go before him to the other side, while he dismissed the crowds. 23 And after he had dismissed the crowds, he went up on the mountain by himself to pray. When evening came, he was there alone, 24 but the boat by this time was many furlongs distant from the land, beaten by the waves; for the wind was against them. 25 And in the fourth watch of the night he came to them, walking on the sea. 26 But when the disciples saw him walking on the sea, they were terrified, saying, "It is a ghost!" And they cried out for fear. 27 But immediately he spoke to them, saying, "Take heart, it is I; have no fear."
28   And Peter answered him, "Lord, if it is you, bid me come to you on the water." 29 He said, "Come." So Peter got out of the boat and walked on the water and came to Jesus; 30 but when he saw the wind, he was afraid, and beginning to sink he cried out, "Lord, save me." 31 Jesus immediately reached out his hand and caught him, saying to him, "O man of little faith, why did you doubt?" 32 And when they got into the boat, the wind ceased. 33 And those in the boat worshipped him, saying, "Truly you are the Son of God."
34   And when they had crossed over, they came to land at Gennesaret. 35 And when the men of that place recognized him, they sent round to all that region and brought to him all that were sick, 36 and besought him that they might only touch the fringe of his garment; and as many as touched it were made well.

The Sea of Galilee is actually a rather small lake (only thirteen by eight miles), which is almost completely surrounded by mountains. When the northern winds are funneled through the mountain peaks, they sweep violently across the lake, causing fierce waves. It was in the midst of such a violent storm that Jesus manifested his power to the disciples by walking on the water.

Just prior to this event, Jesus had performed the miracle of the multiplication of the loaves and fishes. One would think that the disciples, having just seen this demonstration of Jesus' power, would have been confident that Jesus surely could save them from the fury of the storm. Like them, we, too, tend to forget or misunderstand the significance of Jesus' work in our lives.

In this incident, Peter's faith was both tested and strengthened; he experienced the trials and growth of a true disciple of Christ. Having seen the power of Jesus' words and actions, Peter put his faith in him and began to walk across the waves toward Jesus (Matthew 14:29).

By stepping out of the boat at the Lord's invitation, Peter demonstrated at least some degree of realization that Jesus was the Messiah. Even when his faith faltered and he began to sink, it was still to Jesus that he cried out, "Lord, save me" (Matthew 14:30). After the Lord had returned Peter to the safety of the boat, all the disciples worshipped Jesus in awe saying, "Truly you are the Son of God" (14:33).

Day after day, we are confronted with situations that put our faith in the Son of God to the test. Perhaps there has been a sudden death in the family, an unexpected financial burden, or some other crisis in the family that seems too hard to bear. At times like these, our faith may falter; we can doubt that God cares for us or even that he exists. Yet, it is in these very situations that our faith can be strengthened by calling out to Jesus.

"Lord Jesus, in faith we proclaim with all the apostles, 'Truly you are the Son of God.' Through the Holy Spirit, teach us the meaning of this. We trust our lives to you, knowing that our faith will grow as we daily turn to you."

Matthew 15:1-20

[1] Then Pharisees and scribes came to Jesus from Jerusalem and said, [2] "Why do your disciples transgress the tradition of the elders? For they do not wash their hands when they eat." [3] He answered them, "And why do you transgress the commandment of God for the sake of your tradition? [4] For God commanded, 'Honor your father and your mother,' and, 'He who speaks evil of father or mother, let him surely die.' [5] But you say, 'If any one tells his father or his mother, What you would have gained from me is given to God, he need not honor his father.' [6] So, for the sake of your tradition, you have made void the word of God. [7] You hypocrites! Well did Isaiah prophesy of you, when he said: [8] 'This people honors me with their lips, but their heart is far from me; [9] in vain do they worship me, teaching as doctrines the precepts of men.' "
[10] And he called the people to him and said to them, "Hear and understand: [11] not what goes into the mouth defiles a man, but what comes out of the mouth, this defiles a man." [12] Then the disciples came and said to him, "Do you know that the Pharisees were offended when they heard this saying?" [13] He answered, "Every plant which my heavenly Father has not planted will be rooted up. [14] Let them alone; they are blind guides. And if a blind man leads a blind man, both will fall into a pit." [15] But Peter said to him, "Explain the parable to us." [16] And he said, "Are you also still without understanding? [17] Do you not see that whatever goes into

the mouth passes into the stomach, and so passes on? [18] But what comes out of the mouth proceeds from the heart, and this defiles a man. [19] For out of the heart come evil thoughts, murder, adultery, fornication, theft, false witness, slander. [20] These are what defile a man; but to eat with unwashed hands does not defile a man."

Have you ever noticed how radiant people look when they're in love? You can often read what's going on in their hearts just by looking at their faces. In a similar way, our actions often reveal our attitudes. It's not hard to view a person's everyday life and begin to understand how he or she feels about certain political or social issues, or even about God. Some people may be very quiet about their inner lives. But the love and peace of Christ still shine through, whether they're changing a flat tire, buying food at the market, or running a business meeting. Conversely, others may "do" all the right things, but somehow lack the liveliness of a relationship with Christ.

The Pharisees were expert at instituting and adhering to regulations based on ancient traditions. Yet, for some of them, their hearts were far from the God of their ancestors. In a similar way, we may confuse ritual piety with true godliness, or observance of traditions with inner purity. When observance is looked upon as an end in itself, and not as a reflection of love and reverence for God, we have missed out on the life of joy and peace that Jesus promised.

It's easy to believe that a wall of separation exists between our hearts and our bodies, between our inner selves and our actions. But God made us as unified persons, with bodies designed to express what is in our hearts, and hearts intimately tied up with our relationships in the world. God is concerned with our hearts; he takes a deep interest in the way we relate to one another. If we recognize in our relationships toward others harsh words or an angry tongue (see Matthew 15:11), we need to understand that they are reflections of a heart that needs purification by the Lord. If we allow bitterness into our relationships with others, we continue to bring impurity to our hearts.

Jesus said that the greatest commandment is to love God wholeheartedly and to love our neighbor as ourselves (Mark 12:28-31). When such love is our primary concern, we are on the road to purity of heart; we derive life and nourishment from our observances; we relate to others in sincerity and love. Let us ask the Spirit to search us today and help us to see how we can respond to God more deeply and love one another more genuinely.

Matthew 15:21-28

21   And Jesus went away from there and withdrew to the district of Tyre and Sidon. 22 And behold, a Canaanite woman from that region came out and cried, "Have mercy on me, O Lord, Son of David; my daughter is severely possessed by a demon." 23 But he did not answer her a word. And his disciples came and begged him, saying, "Send her away, for she is crying after us." 24 He answered, "I was sent only to the lost sheep of the house of Israel." 25 But she came and knelt before him, saying, "Lord, help me." 26 And he answered, "It is not fair to take the children's bread and throw it to the dogs." 27 She said, "Yes, Lord, yet even the dogs eat the crumbs that fall from their master's table." 28 Then Jesus answered her, "O

woman, great is your faith! Be it done for you as you desire." And her daughter was healed instantly. ❧

The story of the Canaanite woman's faith—a testimony to God's love for all people in all nations—has brought hope and comfort to hurting souls in every age of the church. Many people may wonder: "Is there any hope for me, a sinner? Is there any hope for my son's incurable disease? For my sister who has fallen away from the church? For my co-worker who has never been baptized and did not have a religious upbringing? For everyone who has been traumatized by abuse and neglect?" The answer is found in scripture over and over again: "My house shall be called a house of prayer for *all* peoples" (Isaiah 56:7). No one is excluded.

When this woman heard that Jesus had come to her town, her heart must have leapt in anticipation. She had probably heard stories about his miraculous works, perhaps had heard people say that he was a prophet from God. As she approached him—presumably with a mixture of desperation and hope—she cried out: "Have mercy on me, O Lord, Son of David; my daughter is severely possessed by a demon" (Matthew 15:22). Before making her request, she paid him homage, showing herself to be one of the foreigners who "join themselves to the Lord . . . to love the name of the Lord, and to be his servants" (Isaiah 56:6).

When Jesus told her that he had been sent "only to the lost sheep of the house of Israel" (Matthew 15:24), she pressed on in faith: "Lord, help me . . . even the dogs eat the crumbs that fall from their master's table" (15:25,27). Moved by her humility and her conviction that he could heal her daughter, Jesus rewarded her faith (15:28). Thus it was that an outsider—a Gentile—received the blessings of Yahweh, the God of Israel.

God's power and his desire to bless are not limited to his chosen people; all his promises are still available to us today. We can enter into the healing presence of Jesus as we praise and worship God, imitating the Canaanite woman's adoration. Just as she experienced the Father's loving plan to deliver his people from the enemy, so too can we. With her, let us cry out to the Lord: "Let the peoples praise you, O God; let all the peoples praise you!" (Psalm 67:3).

Matthew 15:29-39

29   And Jesus went on from there and passed along the Sea of Galilee. And he went up on the mountain, and sat down there. 30 And great crowds came to him, bringing with them the lame, the maimed, the blind, the dumb, and many others, and they put them at his feet, and he healed them, 31 so that the throng wondered, when they saw the dumb speaking, the maimed whole, the lame walking, and the blind seeing; and they glorified the God of Israel. 32   Then Jesus called his disciples to him and said, "I have compassion on the crowd, because they have been with me now three days, and have nothing to eat; and I am unwilling to send them away hungry, lest they faint on the way." 33 And the disciples said to him, "Where are we to get bread enough in the desert to feed so great a crowd?" 34 And Jesus said to them, "How many loaves have you?" They said, "Seven, and a few small fish." 35 And commanding the crowd to sit down on the ground, 36 he took the seven loaves and the fish, and having given thanks he broke them

and gave them to the disciples, and the disciples gave them to the crowds. [37] And they all ate and were satisfied; and they took up seven baskets full of the broken pieces left over. [38] Those who ate were four thousand men, besides women and children. [39] And sending away the crowds, he got into the boat and went to the region of Magadan.

The miracles that Jesus performed in his life on earth bore witness both to him and to his Father. They were signs that showed that he was the promised Messiah sent by God. As a result, the people "glorified the God of Israel" (Matthew 15:31). These great events, like the healing of the sick and the feeding of the 4,000, were an invitation to the people to believe.

The Catechism of the Catholic Church points out that the wonders and signs that accompanied Jesus' words revealed that the kingdom of God was present in him. "By freeing some individuals from the earthly evils of hunger, injustice, illness, and death, Jesus performed messianic signs. Nevertheless, he did not come to abolish all evils here below, but to free men from the greatest slavery, sin, which thwarts them in their vocation as God's sons and causes all forms of human bondage" (CCC, 549).

During our lifetime, we may have witnessed miracles ourselves, perhaps the healing of some person who was very ill and not expected to recover. Yet, we also know of cases in which a healing did not occur, even though many people were praying for one.

In these situations, it is helpful to remember that the signs performed by Jesus during his time on earth and the miracles that continue to occur in our own day are only a foreshadowing of what

167

is to come. When Jesus rose from the dead, he healed us all, freeing us from sin and death forever. His compassion for the hungry crowd was only a foretaste of the compassion he has for all humanity, revealed by his willingness to be crucified in order to liberate us from sin.

The ultimate miracle was the resurrection, and all that it did for us. When it is time for us to meet the Lord, we, too, will experience that same miracle of resurrection. In the meantime, Jesus continues to feed us with the bread of life, his body and blood. He strengthens us for the journey here so that we can someday see him face to face.

"Father, thank you for the miracles we have witnessed in our lives. Strengthen our faith so that we can see all the ways in which you care for us. Increase our desire to be fed with the body and blood of your Son, so that we, too, may experience the miracle of eternal life."

Matthew 16:1-12

[1] And the Pharisees and Sadducees came, and to test him they asked him to show them a sign from heaven. [2] He answered them, "When it is evening, you say, 'It will be fair weather; for the sky is red.' [3] And in the morning, 'It will be stormy today, for the sky is red and threatening.' You know how to interpret the appearance of the sky, but you cannot interpret the signs of the times. [4] An evil and adulterous generation seeks for a sign, but no sign shall be given to it except the sign of Jonah." So he left them and departed.
[5] When the disciples reached the other side, they had forgotten to bring any bread. [6] Jesus said to them, "Take heed and beware of

the leaven of the Pharisees and Sadducees." [7] And they discussed it among themselves, saying, "We brought no bread." [8] But Jesus, aware of this, said, "O men of little faith, why do you discuss among yourselves the fact that you have no bread? [9] Do you not yet perceive? Do you not remember the five loaves of the five thousand, and how many baskets you gathered? [10] Or the seven loaves of the four thousand, and how many baskets you gathered? [11] How is it that you fail to perceive that I did not speak about bread? Beware of the leaven of the Pharisees and Sadducees." [12] Then they understood that he did not tell them to beware of the leaven of bread, but of the teaching of the Pharisees and Sadducees.

Because we know Jesus is God, we may tend to overlook the fact that, as a man, he experienced the same human reactions we experience. We may be surprised at the disappointment he expressed when "he sighed deeply in his spirit" (Mark 8:12). But Jesus could read hearts (Luke 9:47); he knew the Pharisees' demand for a sign was born not from a search for truth, but "to test him" (Matthew 16:1). Here, all the synoptic gospel writers reveal Jesus as one like us, even in the frustration brought on by conflicts with unbelieving religious leaders.

In the Old Testament, God strengthened the faith of his people by reminding them of past signs (such as the Exodus), by providing them with signs in the present, and by encouraging them with prophecies of future signs. Many of the people and their leaders expected the messianic days to provide signs and wonders at least equal to those in the Exodus. Such expectations were generally connected with dreams of victory over the pagans.

Jesus may have disappointed such expectations from the human perspective, but he fulfilled them perfectly from the spiritual point of view. He announced the dawning of true salvation by the great sign of his being lifted up in glory on the cross. Unlike the Israelites in the desert, Jesus refused to tempt God by asking for signs on his own account, or to satisfy those who asked for signs in order to test him.

Can we see anything of ourselves in the attitude of those who asked Jesus for a sign? What are our expectations from Jesus' mission? Do we acknowledge his saving death and resurrection as the supreme sign in our lives? Or do we seek to put him to the test by demanding signs that suit us, rather than trusting him and acknowledging our total dependence on him? Do we truly believe his words that the "Father knows what you need before you ask him" (Matthew 6:8)? Do our lives show that kind of trust?

Let us renew our commitment to trust totally in the Father's love, the Son's redeeming sacrifice, and the Spirit's sanctifying work. We need no other sign.

The Messiah Is Revealed

MATTHEW
16:13–17:27

Matthew 16:13-20

13   Now when Jesus came into the district of Caesarea Philippi, he asked his disciples, "Who do men say that the Son of man is?" 14 And they said, "Some say John the Baptist, others say Elijah, and others Jeremiah or one of the prophets." 15 He said to them, "But who do you say that I am?" 16 Simon Peter replied, "You are the Christ, the Son of the living God." 17 And Jesus answered him, "Blessed are you, Simon Bar-Jona! For flesh and blood has not revealed this to you, but my Father who is in heaven. 18 And I tell you, you are Peter, and on this rock I will build my church, and the powers of death shall not prevail against it. 19 I will give you the keys of the kingdom of heaven, and whatever you bind on earth shall be bound in heaven, and whatever you loose on earth shall be loosed in heaven." 20 Then he strictly charged the disciples to tell no one that he was the Christ.

This whole section of Matthew (13:53–17:27) deals with the question of faith and comes to a climax with the proclamation of Jesus as "the Christ, the Son of the living God" (Matthew 16:16). The Hebrew word *Masiah* means "the anointed one"; its Greek translation is *Christos*, from which Jesus receives the title "Christ."

In Matthew's account, Peter used the words "the Son of the living God" to describe Jesus, a phrase not found in Mark's report of this incident (Mark 8:29). Some scripture scholars, comparing these two versions, conjecture that Mark may have preserved Peter's original words while Matthew, drawing on a slightly later, more mature, understanding of the nature of Jesus in the early church, provided the fuller description. This is an important point for us to note: Faith is not static; it is meant to grow and develop and should never become stagnant.

Our own faith must grow to a point where we can make a similar proclamation. It is one thing to recognize Jesus as the Messiah, anointed by God to save his people. But there is a far greater depth involved in understanding Jesus as God, possessing all the transcendent qualities of the godhead, equal in everything to the Father and the Holy Spirit. We could never—in a hundred lifetimes—reach the limits of understanding God. There is always more to learn, more areas in which to grow; and only God can grant us that growth.

Who indeed can fully know the mind of God? What could we ever give him that would lead us to expect anything in return (see Romans 11:34-35)? God is so rich that it is only he who can give us knowledge of who Jesus is, so that we can proclaim him Messiah, the Son of the living God, and more. By the power of the indwelling Holy Spirit, this knowledge should be continually growing and arousing in us a desire to understand him better. The more we understand of our God, the more we will long for the fullness of revelation that will be ours when we are with him for all eternity.

Matthew 16:21-28

²¹ From that time Jesus began to show his disciples that he must go to Jerusalem and suffer many things from the elders and chief priests and scribes, and be killed, and on the third day be raised. ²² And Peter took him and began to rebuke him, saying, "God forbid, Lord! This shall never happen to you." ²³ But he turned and said to Peter, "Get behind me, Satan! You are a hindrance to me; for you are not on the side of God, but of men."

²⁴ Then Jesus told his disciples, "If any man would come after me, let him deny himself and take up his cross and follow me. ²⁵ For whoever would save his life will lose it, and whoever loses his life for my sake will find it. ²⁶ For what will it profit a man, if he gains the whole world and forfeits his life? Or what shall a man give in return for his life? ²⁷ For the Son of man is to come with his angels in the glory of his Father, and then he will repay every man for what he has done. ²⁸ Truly, I say to you, there are some standing here who will not taste death before they see the Son of man coming in his kingdom."

Jesus shocked his disciples when he told them that he must suffer and die in Jerusalem. They simply could not conceive that God would abandon his servant—the one whom Peter had just proclaimed "the Christ, the Son of the living God" (Matthew 16:16). It made no sense! Yet, when Peter tried to dissuade him, Jesus rebuked him sharply: "Get behind me, Satan! You are a hindrance to me; for you are not on the side of God, but of men" (16:23).

Peter was by no means the first (or the last) person who struggled to understand the mind of God. We all tend to view things in human terms. When God called Jeremiah to warn the Israelites about their imminent chastisement, the religious leaders rejected and even physically abused the prophet (Jeremiah 20:1-2). In his confusion, Jeremiah confessed his bitterness: "O Lord, you deceived me, and I was deceived . . . . I have become a laughing-stock all the day" (20:7).

The call to discipleship—which both Peter and Jeremiah experienced—is a privilege and a challenge. The privilege rests in the disciple's close relationship with a loving God. At the last supper, Jesus told his followers: "No longer do I call you servants . . . but I have called you friends, for all that I have heard from my Father I have made known to you" (John 15:15). Imagine the special favor of being known as a friend of God, the grace of learning what is in Jesus' heart as he reveals to you his Father's perfect plan and intention. What could be a greater honor?

The challenge comes as we travel the road that leads to such a relationship with God. Many times, a disciple's limited human wisdom will be confronted by the mystery of divine wisdom. God wants to expand our vision and give us a broader view of the way he works, and this expansion can sometimes be painful. Yet, just as a child sometimes struggles to learn the wiser path from its parents, so too a disciple will gain wisdom as he or she allows God to form a new heart within.

Despite their initial inability to grasp God's ways, both Jeremiah and Peter persisted in obedience. In the end, they became shining beacons reflecting the glory of their beloved Master. The joy and strength God gave them—the intimate knowledge of his love—more than compensated for the cost of discipleship. By allowing God to work in our hearts, we, too, can open a pathway for God to form us as disciples—beloved friends of Jesus Christ.

Matthew 17:1-9

[1] And after six days Jesus took with him Peter and James and John his brother, and led them up a high mountain apart. [2] And he was transfigured before them, and his face shone like the sun, and his garments became white as light. [3] And behold, there appeared to them Moses and Elijah, talking with him. [4] And Peter said to Jesus, "Lord, it is well that we are here; if you wish, I will make three booths here, one for you and one for Moses and one for Elijah." [5] He was still speaking, when lo, a bright cloud overshadowed them, and a voice from the cloud said, "This is my beloved Son, with whom I am well pleased; listen to him." [6] When the disciples heard this, they fell on their faces, and were filled with awe. [7] But Jesus came and touched them, saying, "Rise, and have no fear." [8] And when they lifted up their eyes, they saw no one but Jesus only.

[9] And as they were coming down the mountain, Jesus commanded them, "Tell no one the vision, until the Son of man is raised from the dead." ▨▨▨

The apostles who accompanied Jesus up the mountain to pray were privileged to see Jesus as he would appear for all eternity, after he entered into his glory at the right hand of the Father. The light that transformed Jesus and dazzled the apostles was not a light from outside shining upon him; it came from within, the grace of God, transforming Jesus' human body.

God wants to transform us, just as he transformed his Son; he has "saved us and called us with a holy calling" (2 Timothy 1:9).

Too often, however, we try to change ourselves by using the power of the world to live spiritual lives. It cannot be done that way; it comes only "through the appearing of our Savior Christ Jesus, who abolished death and brought life and immortality to light through the gospel" (2 Timothy 1:10). As we come to see Jesus through the eyes of faith, his Spirit is able to work within us, transforming our lives and giving us a share in his perfect holiness.

The transformation God wants to work in us is not merely for our own well-being. All members of the church of Christ are meant to reflect his glory and, by this reflection, to change the world. By the power of his Spirit, the Father wants to transform us all into radiant sons and daughters, shining like the sun in this darkened world. Ever since his first promise to Abram, that he would make of him "a great nation" (Genesis 12:2), God has been working to bring his people to that fullness of life that will renew the face of the earth. The degree to which we are transformed and empowered is the degree to which we will be effective in convincing the world of the glory of Christ and the truth of his salvation.

Jesus' transfiguration helped prepare the apostles for the salvation he was to win for all humanity. Our transformation—and the transformation of the church—can prepare the world to receive and accept the salvation Jesus has won for us. We must let the Holy Spirit work through us, molding us into the image of Christ. As we are transformed, the church will reflect God's glory, and the whole world will be touched.

Matthew 17:10-13

¹⁰ And the disciples asked him, "Then why do the scribes say that first Elijah must come?" ¹¹ He replied, "Elijah does come, and he is to restore all things; ¹² but I tell you that Elijah has already come, and they did not know him, but did to him whatever they pleased. So also the Son of man will suffer at their hands." ¹³ Then the disciples understood that he was speaking to them of John the Baptist.

This conversation took place immediately after Jesus' transfiguration, when the disciples had seen Elijah with Jesus. The prophet Malachi said that there would be a forerunner to announce this time of God's intervention in human history: "Behold, I send my messenger to prepare the way before me, and the Lord whom you seek will suddenly come to his temple" (Malachi 3:1); and, "Behold, I will send you Elijah the prophet before the great and terrible day of the Lord comes. And he will turn the hearts of fathers to their children and the hearts of children to their fathers" (4:5-6).

During this time in Israel, there was widespread messianic speculation, coupled with dreams of temporal glory for Israel. The Jews had a hope, rooted in the scriptures, that God would carry out his plan to save his people, and that his instrument would be the Messiah, the Son of David.

Jesus told his disciples that this prophecy had already been fulfilled in the person of John the Baptist. When John's birth was foretold to his father, Zechariah, the angel Gabriel declared that

John would "go before him in the spirit and power of Elijah, to turn the hearts of the fathers to the children" (Luke 1:17).

The people did not recognize John the Baptist as the new Elijah and, consequently, would not acknowledge Jesus as the promised Messiah. Reading this passage today, we might marvel at the shortsightedness of Jesus' contemporaries. But the word of God confronts us with the same question that perplexed the people of Jesus' time: "Who do you say Jesus is?" (see Matthew 16:13). If he is merely a model to emulate, then he will not be vital to our lives. But if we say that he is truly the Messiah, whose death and resurrection has saved us, then the only possible response is to commit our lives to him.

"Father, we confess our inability to recognize your Son Jesus Christ as our Savior. We surrender ourselves to him and ask the indwelling Spirit to prepare our hearts to receive him in a deeper way."

Matthew 17:14-21

[14] And when they came to the crowd, a man came up to him and kneeling before him said, [15] "Lord, have mercy on my son, for he is an epileptic and he suffers terribly; for often he falls into the fire, and often into the water. [16] And I brought him to your disciples, and they could not heal him." [17] And Jesus answered, "O faithless and perverse generation, how long am I to be with you? How long am I to bear with you? Bring him here to me." [18] And Jesus rebuked him, and the demon came out of him, and the boy was cured instantly. [19] Then the disciples came to Jesus privately and said, "Why could we not cast it out?" [20] He said to them, "Because of your little faith. For truly, I say to you, if you have faith as a grain of mustard seed, you will say to this mountain, 'Move from here to there,' and it will move; and nothing will be impossible to you. [21] [But this kind never comes out except by prayer and fasting.]"

If you have faith as a grain of mustard seed. (Matthew 17:20)

Most of us would say we have faith—that is, we believe in God. The problem usually is that we fail to apply what faith we have to our daily circumstances. When problems arise (poor health, death of a loved one, loss of a job), we begin to grow fearful. Then we begin to doubt and question. Does God really love us? Is he truly dwelling in us, as he promised, allowing us to share his divine life? In times of trial, we tend to rely more on the seen than the unseen, and this is the opposite of faith. As a consequence, we are often overwhelmed by our problems. We show signs of "little faith."

We are not alone in this problem. Jesus' disciples also suffered from "little faith" (Matthew 17:20). In their lives, they had come to a point of following Jesus, but not to a point of sufficiently trusting in him. This is similar to our situation when we believe in God, but do not entrust our lives to him.

Even a kernel of faith can produce great results. This is what Jesus meant when he said: "If you have faith as a grain of mustard seed, you will say to this mountain, 'Move from here to there,' and it will move" (Matthew 17:20). To have such faith, and for that faith to grow robust, we must cultivate it. Since "faith is the assurance of things hoped for, the conviction of things not seen" (Hebrews 11:1), we need to do things, such as pray, which make us aware of unseen realities. Mother Teresa said: "Has your faith grown? If you do not pray, your faith will leave you" (*Total Surrender*, p. 99).

Prayer helps us grow in faith by turning our attention to Jesus, not to ourselves—by focusing us on his promises, not on our own feelings. It helps us to have "conviction of things not seen" and to ask for the grace to trust in him. Let us pray for a deeper faith: "Lord Jesus, help us set our hearts on things above, to turn to you constantly as the source of all life. Renew us by the power of your Spirit and give us faith, even if only the size of a mustard seed."

Matthew 17:22-27

22 As they were gathering in Galilee, Jesus said to them, "The Son of man is to be delivered into the hands of men, 23 and they will kill him, and he will be raised on the third day." And they were greatly distressed.

24 When they came to Capernaum, the collectors of the half-shekel tax went up to Peter and said, "Does not your teacher pay the tax?" 25 He said, "Yes." And when he came home, Jesus spoke to him first, saying, "What do you think, Simon? From whom do kings of the earth take toll or tribute? From their sons or from others?" 26 And when he said, "From others," Jesus said to him, "Then the sons are free. 27 However, not to give offense to them, go to the sea and cast a hook, and take the first fish that comes up, and when you open its mouth you will find a shekel; take that and give it to them for me and for yourself." ※※※

Matthew was focusing on the way in which the disciples were coming to know who Jesus really was (Matthew 13:53–17:27). They had seen this man feed multitudes of people from a few loaves and fishes (14:13-21); they had seen him walk on water (14:26); they had witnessed physical healings of multitudes of people who were sick (14:34-36); and had seen a demon cast out of the afflicted (17:14-20).

As if this were not enough, Peter, James, and John saw Jesus transfigured on a mountain top and heard the voice of God proclaiming: "This is my beloved Son" (Matthew 17:5). Through these signs and actions, the disciples came to believe that Jesus was the

Messiah, the Son of God, who had come to save the people. Jesus confirmed the reality of who he was by his words to his disciples.

The passion prediction and the story of the paying of the temple tax gave the disciples two clear indications of Jesus' identity (Matthew 17:22-23,24-27). First of all, Jesus proclaimed himself to be the "Son of man," which was a reference to Daniel's vision of a heavenly being who was given "dominion and glory and kingdom, that all peoples, nations and languages should serve him" (Daniel 7:14).

Jesus then compared himself with the children of kings who are not obligated to pay taxes to their father (Matthew 17:25). Therefore, Jesus didn't have to pay the religious tax for the upkeep of the temple because he was the Son of him whose temple it was! Thus, Jesus was more than just a healer or a preacher; more than just a miracle worker. He was, and is, the Son of man, destined to reign over all people forever; he was, and is, the Son of almighty God.

Let us come to know Jesus in an ever deeper way. Let us look to Jesus in our liturgies, our prayer, and our reading of the scriptures, asking for revelation about who he is and knowing confidently that he wants to reveal himself to us, just as he did to his apostles.

"Jesus, we want to know you better. Reveal to us your greatness and glory as the Son of man and the Son of God. We want to be your disciples and follow you."

Discourse on the Church

MATTHEW
18

Matthew 18:1-11

¹   At that time the disciples came to Jesus, saying, "Who is the greatest in the kingdom of heaven?" ² And calling to him a child, he put him in the midst of them, ³ and said, "Truly, I say to you, unless you turn and become like children, you will never enter the kingdom of heaven. ⁴ Whoever humbles himself like this child, he is the greatest in the kingdom of heaven.

⁵   "Whoever receives one such child in my name receives me; ⁶ but whoever causes one of these little ones who believe in me to sin, it would be better for him to have a great millstone fastened round his neck and to be drowned in the depth of the sea.

⁷   "Woe to the world for temptations to sin! For it is necessary that temptations come, but woe to the man by whom the temptation comes! ⁸ And if your hand or your foot causes you to sin, cut it off and throw it away; it is better for you to enter life maimed or lame than with two hands or two feet to be thrown into the eternal fire. ⁹ And if your eye causes you to sin, pluck it out and throw it away; it is better for you to enter life with one eye than with two eyes to be thrown into the hell of fire.

¹⁰   "See that you do not despise one of these little ones; for I tell you that in heaven their angels always behold the face of my Father who is in heaven. ¹¹[For the Son of man came to save the lost."]

Unless you turn and become like children,
you will never enter the kingdom of heaven. (Matthew 18:3)

Jesus was not speaking about being childish; he was speaking about being humble and turning to God in trust, as one would turn to a kind and loving father. In a humble relationship with

God, one would find qualities such as trust, admiration and confidence. One would also experience a desire to please God as well as to be in his presence, knowing and believing that he cares about our needs, desires, and our search for happiness. This is the relationship that exists between children and parents.

One of the most important aspects of this humble relationship with the Father is that we *turn* from our proud ways and *change*. We need to go to our Father like the prodigal son and say, "Father, I have sinned against heaven and before you; I am no longer worthy to be called your son" (Luke 15:21). As we recognize that God is our loving Father and confess our sins to him with truthfulness and sorrow, we will be on the path toward humility.

The tendency of the world is to scorn the humble; that is why Jesus warned, "See that you do not despise one of these little ones" (Matthew 18:10). But God loves the humble; that is why Jesus made this promise: "Blessed are the poor in spirit, for theirs is the kingdom of heaven" (5:3). God wants all of his disciples to be like trusting children, for his desire is that none should be lost. "It is not the will of my Father who is in heaven that one of these little ones should perish" (18:14).

Let us pray today that we will seek to develop a spirit of humility in our lives. Examine your conscience and ask God's forgiveness for the ways in which you are not humble. Beg the Holy Spirit to reveal to you areas of pride and arrogance and to teach you how to be humble before God and before the world. Tell your loving Father that you want to be like a little child in his eyes so that you can enter into his kingdom.

Matthew 18:12-14

[12] "What do you think? If a man has a hundred sheep, and one of them has gone astray, does he not leave the ninety-nine on the mountains and go in search of the one that went astray? [13] And if he finds it, truly, I say to you, he rejoices over it more than over the ninety-nine that never went astray. [14] So it is not the will of my Father who is in heaven that one of these little ones should perish."

> *The whole of human nature is a single sheep*
> *and you [Jesus] took it upon your shoulders.*
> (St. Gregory of Nyssa, On the Canticle of Canticles)

We are the sheep and Jesus is the Good Shepherd. Whether we realize it or not, we were born into a life separated from God (Romans 3:10-18). We are all lost sheep, damaged by sin, and in need of healing. If not dealt with, this inherited tendency to sin can plunge us into a most perilous situation. Our own green pastures—things, places, or positions that look so good to us—ultimately leave us empty, lonely, and unfulfilled if they are not from God. Why is this so? Because God has put within us a desire for him and this desire can be satisfied by nothing other than himself. His will is that we experience the green pastures *he* has in store for us, much different than the ones *we* might choose out of our fallen natures.

Jesus redeemed and ransomed us by an act of divine mercy. He left his throne to come and save us, to free us, to give us a whole new life with him. We should cherish the new life he offers us because it was purchased at the price of his suffering, his death, and his blood!

From the beginning of time, God has wanted to gather a people to himself. The image of the shepherd is used frequently to describe God leading his people from slavery to freedom. God called the people of Israel to be his own. Now, in Christ Jesus, he gathers the Israel of God (Galatians 6:16) from all peoples and nations. His intention is that there be one flock and one shepherd (John 10:16).

The return of the stray sheep pleases God who wishes for none to be lost. Let us pray that all people will come to know the love and mercy of the Good Shepherd, especially those friends and loved ones who have gone astray. Even now, God is pursuing them and pouring out his grace to them. He wants his flock to be complete.

"Loving Shepherd, gather us to be your own. May none of us resist your call and remain apart from you."

Matthew 18:15-20

15 "If your brother sins against you, go and tell him his fault, between you and him alone. If he listens to you, you have gained your brother. 16 But if he does not listen, take one or two others along with you, that every word may be confirmed by the evidence of two or three witnesses. 17 If he refuses to listen to them, tell it to the church; and if he refuses to listen even to the church, let him be to you as a Gentile and a tax collector. 18 Truly, I say to you, whatever you bind on earth shall be bound in heaven, and whatever you loose on earth shall be loosed in heaven. 19 Again I say to you, if two of you agree on earth about anything they ask, it will be done for them by my Father in heaven. 20 For where two or three are gathered in my name, there am I in the midst of them."

God created us in love, and it is this very love that he wants to pour into our hearts. Because we are his people—the "sheep of his hand" (Psalm 95:7)—God leads us, guides us, and disciplines us out of love. We are the delight of his heart, and all his works—his provisions, his compassion, and his discipline — are intended to lead us back to him.

Out of this same heart of love, Jesus calls us to help our brothers and sisters—to seek the best for them and to lead them back to the Father. Sometimes this may include saying things that are difficult in order to protect and nurture their relationship with God. As hard as this may be, the debt of love that we owe one another in Christ compels us (Romans 13:8). We love because Christ first loved us; out of this love, we seek to build one another up in the

Lord. Without the love of Christ, we risk speaking out of self-righteousness, judgmentalism or feelings of superiority. We can easily understand how such correction could result in hurt and shame.

It is not unusual that parents sometimes have to say difficult things to their children in order to help them grow. Most parents recognize the challenge of correcting out of love rather than out of frustration or anger. The goal of parenting is to guide our children to Christian adulthood so that they can receive their full inheritance and rights as children of God. In the same way, God loves and disciplines us—his beloved children.

God created us to live in unity with him and with each other. We can know this unity because God's only begotten Son removed every dividing wall by his death on the cross. Through the gift of the Spirit, he has given us everything we need to live out this unity—to become vessels of his love and mercy. Let us pray for the grace to serve one another in love, knowing that such service gives joy to our heavenly Father's heart.

"Father, may the unity that Jesus won for us on the cross be at the center of our hearts as we serve others in your name. Help us love one another with the same love you have shown us."

Matthew 18:21-35

[21] Then Peter came up and said to him, "Lord, how often shall my brother sin against me, and I forgive him? As many as seven times?" [22] Jesus said to him, "I do not say to you seven times, but seventy times seven.

[23] "Therefore the kingdom of heaven may be compared to a king who wished to settle accounts with his servants. [24] When he began the reckoning, one was brought to him who owed him ten thousand talents; [25] and as he could not pay, his lord ordered him to be sold, with his wife and children and all that he had, and payment to be made. [26] So the servant fell on his knees, imploring him, 'Lord, have patience with me, and I will pay you everything.' [27] And out of pity for him the lord of that servant released him and forgave him the debt. [28] But that same servant, as he went out, came upon one of his fellow servants who owed him a hundred denarii; and seizing him by the throat he said, 'Pay what you owe.' [29] So his fellow servant fell down and besought him, 'Have patience with me, and I will pay you.' [30] He refused and went and put him in prison till he should pay the debt. [31] When his fellow servants saw what had taken place, they were greatly distressed, and they went and reported to their lord all that had taken place. [32] Then his lord summoned him and said to him, 'You wicked servant! I forgave you all that debt because you besought me; [33] and should not you have had mercy on your fellow servant, as I had mercy on you?' [34] And in anger his lord delivered him to the jailers, till he should pay all his debt. [35] So also my heavenly Father will do to every one of you, if you do not forgive your brother from your heart."

Jesus taught us to pray to the Father with these words: "Forgive us our debts, as we also have forgiven our debtors" (Matthew 6:12). These words challenge the Christian community to grapple with the practical questions of forgiveness and church order.

Perhaps only an accountant would tend to look at this parable of the two servants and consider the amounts of the debts owed. Such a consideration, however, does lead us to a startling discovery: One hundred denarii represented a laborer's wages for 100 *days* of work. Ten thousand talents were equivalent to 150,000 *years'* wages, about half-a-million times greater. The figure need not be taken literally: The numbers indicate how small the second servant's debt was in comparison with the first; they also reveal the immensity of the debt that the first servant owed to his king, a debt that could never have been repaid, even with the greatest enterprise.

While the number and nature of our sins may differ, it is an unfortunate fact that all of us commit sins that hurt ourselves and others. Our human tendency is to point to the wrong that has been done to us, and never to forget it: "He did this." "She said that." "It's unfair and it hurt me." Even small children can recount such experiences in their young lives.

In teaching us to forgive our brothers and sisters, Jesus was not glossing over the reality of the hurts that sinful actions cause. It's just that a higher reality—God's forgiveness of our sins—should enable us to forgive those who offend us. Compared to our offenses against God, the debt owed us is comparatively minor. It is simple justice that we should forgive without limit. Ben Sira saw this truth from afar when he said: "Forgive your neighbor the wrong he has done, and then your sins will be pardoned when you pray" (Sirach 28:2).

Consider the words of C.S. Lewis, a noted Christian essayist of this century:

To forgive the incessant provocations of daily life—
to keep on forgiving the bossy mother-in-law, the bullying

husband, the nagging wife, the selfish daughter, the deceitful son—how can we do it? Only, I think, by meaning our words when we say in our prayers each night: "Forgive us our trespasses as we forgive those that trespass against us." We are offered forgiveness on no other terms. To refuse to do it is to refuse God's mercy on ourselves (*The Weight of Glory*, "On Forgiveness," p. 7).

A Devotional Commentary on Matthew

The Journey Toward Jerusalem

MATTHEW
19–20

Matthew 19:1-12

[1] Now when Jesus had finished these sayings, he went away from Galilee and entered the region of Judea beyond the Jordan; [2] and large crowds followed him, and he healed them there.

[3] And Pharisees came up to him and tested him by asking, "Is it lawful to divorce one's wife for any cause?" [4] He answered, "Have you not read that he who made them from the beginning made them male and female, [5] and said, 'For this reason a man shall leave his father and mother and be joined to his wife, and the two shall become one flesh'? [6] So they are no longer two but one flesh. What therefore God has joined together, let no man put asunder." [7] They said to him, "Why then did Moses command one to give a certificate of divorce, and to put her away?" [8] He said to them, "For your hardness of heart Moses allowed you to divorce your wives, but from the beginning it was not so. [9] And I say to you: whoever divorces his wife, except for unchastity, and marries another, commits adultery; and he who marries a divorced woman, commits adultery."

[10] The disciples said to him, "If such is the case of a man with his wife, it is not expedient to marry." [11] But he said to them, "Not all men can receive this saying, but only those to whom it is given. [12] For there are eunuchs who have been so from birth, and there are eunuchs who have been made eunuchs by men, and there are eunuchs who have made themselves eunuchs for the sake of the kingdom of heaven. He who is able to receive this, let him receive it."

Unless you turn and become like children, you will never enter the kingdom of heaven. (Matthew 18:3)

Leaving Galilee and returning to the region of Judea, Jesus took another step on the road to his passion and death. In Galilee, he had revealed the power of God in signs and wonders and clear teaching. In Judea, he was to be tested by the Pharisees and scribes who would try to trick him. Even so, he continued to heal and bring the good news of God's love to the people. As Jesus traveled toward and entered into Jerusalem, he continued to form his disciples as he invited them to life in him (Matthew 19:1–22:46).

Some Pharisees tried to use the question of divorce as a way of discrediting Jesus. Even today we see how we might try to use controversial subjects to entrap those with whom we disagree. While this sort of thing commonly takes place on the political battlefield, if we look into our own hearts, we will discover that this type of action is not beyond any of us. Without the Holy Spirit to prod our consciences, we can be every bit as cynical as these Pharisees.

The question of divorce is often painful, so it is important to remember that Jesus' intent was not to cause pain but to set a clear and godly plan for human relationships. Jesus referred the Pharisees to the creation story and God's original intent for man and woman (Matthew 19:4-6). They were to be united in a covenant relationship between God and his people. Unfortunately, this vision is often negatively affected by the selfishness and even evil lurking in the human heart. Personal efforts alone—no matter how important and sincere they are—can never attain this high ideal. Marital love and stability requires faith and obedience to the Father whose desire is to transform us by the work of Christ.

As followers of Jesus, let us pray that we will be able to embrace the life of Christ and follow in his footsteps—the way of love and obedience. God is faithful. No matter what our circumstances may be, if we turn to him, he will hear our prayer and show us the way.

"Heavenly Father, cleanse our hearts and purify our consciences. Protect the sanctity of the family and help those struggling or suffering in their marriages and family life."

Matthew 19:13-15

13 Then children were brought to him that he might lay his hands on them and pray. The disciples rebuked the people; 14 but Jesus said, "Let the children come to me, and do not hinder them; for to such belongs the kingdom of heaven." 15 And he laid his hands on them and went away.

Let the children come to me, and do not hinder them.
(Matthew 19:14)

From the time of the patriarchs, Jewish parents always brought their children to the elders of the faith for a blessing. Jesus' disciples, perhaps to save him from what they saw as an annoyance and an interruption of his work, attempted to turn the children away. Once again, Jesus showed that our ways are not his ways. He commanded that the children be brought to him.

The new life of God given to each child at baptism requires careful nurturing, much as a seed needs the right conditions to foster healthy growth. A child's faith can be damaged by poor example, lack of teaching, or inadequate training. The new life can be choked out when parents allow the spirit of the world to infringe upon their own spiritual lives. Confusion is sown in the child's mind when those whom he or she admires and respects convey the impression that worldly renown or material success is more important than a relationship with Jesus. If our homes are not places where Jesus is welcomed, the trust that small children may have in the Lord is quickly lost as they mature.

How different the results when we bring our children to Jesus! Our children are entrusted to us by God and he has promised to work within each of them, "for to such belongs the kingdom of heaven" (Matthew 19:14). Our part is to bring them to Jesus, no matter what their age. Our chief aim must be that our children come to know the Lord. In order for this to happen, we have to take the time to teach them about Jesus and the scriptures. We must train them in God's ways and teach them about the church Christ established. Instead of forcing "religion" on them, we should ask God to show us how to win their hearts to him. Through our own prayer and example, our sons and daughters will come to desire the life of Christ.

"Father, we realize that each child is your special creation; each belongs to you more than to us. Give us the wisdom to be able to bring them to your Son, Jesus. Send the Holy Spirit to purify our hearts so that we can lead faith-filled lives that will be an effective witness to the young."

Matthew 19:16-22

[16] And behold, one came up to him, saying, "Teacher, what good deed must I do, to have eternal life?" [17] And he said to him, "Why do you ask me about what is good? One there is who is good. If you would enter life, keep the commandments." [18] He said to him, "Which?" And Jesus said, "You shall not kill, You shall not commit adultery, You shall not steal, You shall not bear false witness, [19] Honor your father and mother, and, You shall love your neighbor as yourself." [20] The young man said to him, "All these I have observed; what do I still lack?" [21] Jesus said to him, "If you would be perfect, go, sell what you possess and give to the poor, and you will have treasure in heaven; and come, follow me." [22] When the young man heard this he went away sorrowful; for he had great possessions.

A young man encountering Jesus asked: "What good deed must I do, to have eternal life?" He was obviously looking for some activity, some additional conformity to the law in which he could engage to ensure his desired end. Perhaps he sensed in his heart that something more was required of him than mere observance of the commandments, to which he had been constantly faithful (Matthew 19:16,20). Jesus' gracious response was an invitation to perfection. He invited the young man to share discipleship, with all the insecurity that goes with the voluntary giving up of material wealth to live as Jesus and his first disciples lived (19:21-22).

The intimate following of Jesus—to which each of us is called

—requires that we detach ourselves from anything that could prevent us from giving ourselves to the service of Jesus and our neighbor. This could mean money, career, talents, or social standing—anything that might deter us from making God our first priority.

Dorothy Day, an outspoken Catholic activist of this century, dedicated herself to the care of the poor and the destitute in fifty Houses of Hospitality she founded during her lifetime. She heard the call of the gospel and, unencumbered by wealth or the desire for earthly goods, was able to respond wholeheartedly. Speaking of the poverty that frees, she wrote:

> It is voluntary poverty which needs to be preached to the comfortable congregations . . . . A readiness for poverty, a disposition to accept it, is enough to begin with. We will always get what we need. "Take no thought for what you shall eat or drink—the Lord knows you have need of these things." (*Meditations of Dorothy Day*, p. 63)

We have all heard the call to follow Jesus. What is our response? Do we believe that as we detach ourselves from the things of this world God will care for us and the treasure of heaven will fulfill us? Let us ask God to prepare our hearts, for before there can be action, there must be conviction. "Loving Father, prepare my heart that I may loose my grasp on the things of this world to follow Jesus more perfectly."

Matthew 19:23-30

²³ And Jesus said to his disciples, "Truly, I say to you, it will be hard for a rich man to enter the kingdom of heaven. ²⁴ Again I tell you, it is easier for a camel to go through the eye of a needle than for a rich man to enter the kingdom of God." ²⁵ When the disciples heard this they were greatly astonished, saying, "Who then can be saved?" ²⁶ But Jesus looked at them and said to them, "With men this is impossible, but with God all things are possible." ²⁷ Then Peter said in reply, "Lo, we have left everything and followed you. What then shall we have?" ²⁸ Jesus said to them, "Truly, I say to you, in the new world, when the Son of man shall sit on his glorious throne, you who have followed me will also sit on twelve thrones, judging the twelve tribes of Israel. ²⁹ And every one who has left houses or brothers or sisters or father or mother or children or lands, for my name's sake, will receive a hundredfold, and inherit eternal life. ³⁰ But many that are first will be last, and the last first."

Wealth of itself is not evil, and references to the dangers of wealth in both the Old and New Testaments refer to an attitude toward riches that denies God his proper place of authority in our lives (Isaiah 2:7; Proverbs 11:28; 1 John 2:15). This is what Jesus was telling the disciples about the difficulty of the rich entering God's kingdom and the rewards that belong to those who give God his rightful place (Matthew 19:24,28-29).

The disciples "were greatly astonished, saying, 'Who then can be saved?' " (Matthew 19:25). Perhaps the same anxiety echoes in our hearts since the warning strikes at the practice of seeking security from our possessions, whether they be great or small. We so readily become possessive, so easily forgetting that all we have is a gift from God. We are only stewards of God's riches, which are all meant to be used for the service and the good of others (1 Peter 4:10).

In his desire for our wholehearted love, Jesus invites us to take a closer look at the question of wealth. He does not want us to be filled with fear at the prospect of losing our material possessions, but to concentrate on the spiritual riches he offers us. God has promised to provide for our every need, but we can't begin to experience his divine providence until we heed Jesus' admonitions about wealth. We must ask the Holy Spirit to help us recognize that nothing material—neither money, talents, level of education, social standing, or possessions—can fully satisfy us or buy the happiness and salvation Jesus came to bring. There is something far greater than all the goods of this world that we so love and cherish. It is the eternal richness of Christ.

Our attachment to worldly things may make this seem impossible, but Jesus has the answer: "With men, this is impossible, but with God all things are possible" (Matthew 19:26). The rewards for those who accept Jesus' invitation are beyond comprehension (1 Corinthians 2:9). But we won't appreciate those rewards and we won't even know what is possible unless we trust God and begin to act.

"Holy Spirit, we believe that with God all things are possible. Change our hearts so that God alone may be our true treasure."

Matthew 20:1-16

[1] "For the kingdom of heaven is like a householder who went out early in the morning to hire laborers for his vineyard. [2] After agreeing with the laborers for a denarius a day, he sent them into his vineyard. [3] And going out about the third hour he saw others standing idle in the market place; [4] and to them he said, 'You go into the vineyard too, and whatever is right I will give you.' So they went. [5] Going out again about the sixth hour and the ninth hour, he did the same. [6] And about the eleventh hour he went out and found others standing; and he said to them, 'Why do you stand here idle all day?' [7] They said to him, 'Because no one has hired us.' He said to them, 'You go into the vineyard too.' [8] And when evening came, the owner of the vineyard said to his steward, 'Call the laborers and pay them their wages, beginning with the last, up to the first.' [9] And when those hired about the eleventh hour came, each of them received a denarius. [10] Now when the first came, they thought they would receive more; but each of them also received a denarius. [11] And on receiving it they grumbled at the householder, [12] saying, 'These last worked only one hour, and you have made them equal to us who have borne the burden of the day and the scorching heat.' [13] But he replied to one of them, 'Friend, I am doing you no wrong; did you not agree with me for a denarius? [14] Take what belongs to you, and go; I choose to give to this last as I give to you. [15] Am I not allowed to do what I choose with what belongs to me? Or do you begrudge my generosity?' [16] So the last will be first, and the first last."

I magine working an entire day for the same pay as a person who worked only for one hour. Our sense of justice would be outraged. Seen through the filter of the world—its concerns and rules of fairness—it is easy to side with the laborers in this parable who thought that, since they had worked more, they would be paid more. It's fair. It's right. Those first hirelings started about 6:00 A.M. They toiled nearly twelve hours in the heat and sun for one denarius, a silver Roman coin typically valued at a day's work. The last laborers worked about an hour late in the day and received the same wage.

It's natural to think this way, but what we fail to consider is that Jesus was telling a parable about the kingdom of God. Fairness isn't an issue. None of us deserves anything from God; none of us could ever cause him to be indebted to us. Everything we have, even life itself, is a free gift graciously bestowed on us. We never could have earned the right of relating personally to God. In serving him, we receive much more than we ever give him. Working in the vineyard, in God's kingdom, is not a burden but a privilege! If we have responded early, we are not unfortunate or ill-used; we are favored. If we have responded late, we are favored too!

St. Teresa of Avila expressed it this way: "We should forget the number of years we have served him, for the sum total of all we can do is worthless by comparison with a single drop of the blood which the Lord shed for us The more we serve him, the more deeply we fall into his debt" (*Life*, 39).

Jesus told this parable of the workers in the vineyard as he journeyed to Jerusalem, where he was to be crucified. His death and resurrection transformed the world, filling it with his love. When we know and follow Jesus, we will also know the privilege of serving unreservedly in his vineyard.

"Jesus, enkindle in our hearts the love that drove you to the cross. Inflame us with the desire to serve long and devotedly in your vineyard, and deliver us from the error of comparing our service with that of others you have called."

Matthew 20:17-28

[17] And as Jesus was going up to Jerusalem, he took the twelve disciples aside, and on the way he said to them, [18] "Behold, we are going up to Jerusalem; and the Son of man will be delivered to the chief priests and scribes, and they will condemn him to death, [19] and deliver him to the Gentiles to be mocked and scourged and crucified, and he will be raised on the third day." [20] Then the mother of the sons of Zebedee came up to him, with her sons, and kneeling before him she asked him for something. [21] And he said to her, "What do you want?" She said to him, "Command that these two sons of mine may sit, one at your right hand and one at your left, in your kingdom." [22] But Jesus answered, "You do not know what you are asking. Are you able to drink the cup that I am to drink?" They said to him, "We are able." [23] He said to them, "You will drink my cup, but to sit at my right hand and at my left is not mine to grant, but it is for those for whom it has been prepared by my Father." [24] And when the ten heard it, they were indignant at the two brothers. [25] But Jesus called them to him and said, "You know that the rulers of the Gentiles lord it over them, and their great men exercise authority over them. [26] It shall not be so among you; but whoever would be great among you must be your servant, [27] and whoever would be first among you must be your slave; [28] even as the Son of man came not to be served but to serve, and to give his life as a ransom for many."

Jesus knew that the cross was at the heart of his mission as Savior. He had spoken several times to the apostles about his journey to Jerusalem and his death on the cross (Matthew 16:21; 17:22-23; 20:17-19), but they did not understand the meaning of his words. And so he spoke again, as clearly as possible, about his impending death and his resurrection from the dead (20:28).

The story of the mother of James and John asking for places of honor for her sons not only demonstrates the general lack of understanding among his followers, but teaches the importance of the cross as well. Jesus asked them if they could drink the cup of suffering. To their positive response, he gave assurance that they would indeed drink the bitter cup of his cross, for only those who take up the cross of Jesus can triumph (Matthew 20:22-23).

Just as the cross was central to Jesus' life, so must it be central to the lives of his followers. The prospect of this may leave us bewildered and fearful, just as Jesus' prediction to his apostles left them wondering whether or not they could endure what lay ahead for them.

St. Teresa of Avila (1515-1582) said that when Jesus asks us (as he did James and John) if we can drink of his chalice, we should reply, "We can." Teresa said that it is "quite right to do so, for his Majesty gives strength to those who, he sees, have need of it, and he defends these souls in every way" (*Interior Castle*, "Sixth Mansions," XI). This promise should fill us with hope and courage in the face of whatever Jesus may demand of us. Through his grace, we can live in obedience to the Father, just as Jesus did.

Jesus came "not to be served but to serve" (Matthew 20:28). This is one way we can partake of his cup—the cup of generous service to others. If we are to be followers of Jesus, we need to be more and more concerned with and responsive to the needs of others—in the family, the parish, at work or at school—and less occupied with our own selfish needs. From the cross we can gain the necessary strength to remain steadfast in doing this and so come one day to the glory Jesus won for us through his victory on the cross.

Matthew 20:29-34

²⁹ And as they went out of Jericho, a great crowd followed him. ³⁰ And behold, two blind men sitting by the roadside, when they heard that Jesus was passing by, cried out, "Have mercy on us, Son of David!" ³¹ The crowd rebuked them, telling them to be silent; but they cried out the more, "Lord, have mercy on us, Son of David!" ³² And Jesus stopped and called them, saying, "What do you want me to do for you?" ³³ They said to him, "Lord, let our eyes be opened." ³⁴ And Jesus in pity touched their eyes, and immediately they received their sight and followed him.

A blind beggar squatting by the roadside was probably a familiar sight to the people of Jericho or to pilgrims on the road to Jerusalem. Such a scene might evoke little attention or sympathy from passers-by. These two beggars, however, though physically blind, were far more perceptive spiritually than many of those who made up this crowd of Passover pilgrims, for "when they heard that Jesus was passing by, cried out, 'Have mercy on us, Son of David! ' " (Matthew 20:30). They were not intimidated by efforts to silence them (20:31).

Despite the noise generated by the crowd, Jesus heard and recognized this earnest cry of faith. He called to them and they responded eagerly. When the Lord asked what they wanted, they replied: "Lord, let our eyes be opened" (Matthew 20:33). Immediately, touched with pity and compassion, Jesus restored their sight. They threw aside the hopelessness of their old life of begging and followed Jesus (20:34).

Like these blind beggars, we need to throw off the cloak of our old ways of life. We need new life to be able to respond to Jesus' call to follow his way in faith. We all have our own situations of seeming hopelessness—patterns of sin, marital problems, family or business difficulties—but first we have to recognize our need for healing. We must believe that Jesus is the only answer to each and every one of our needs; we must cry out repeatedly with faith in his healing power.

Too often, we first try all other possible means, our own ingenuity or power of persuasion, every ploy of human logic to ameliorate situations. Only when all else has failed do we turn to God. God *wants* us to seek his help. He wants us to realize that in the cross of Christ is the power for us to be filled with new life. By the saving death of Jesus, we have been freed for discipleship. His precious blood has the power to remove whatever might hinder our wholehearted response.

Today in prayer, ask Jesus to show you the darkness that prevents your knowing, loving, and following him more faithfully. Cry out in faith: "Lord Jesus, let me see again!"

Jesus in Jerusalem

MATTHEW
21–23

Matthew 21:1-11

[1] And when they drew near to Jerusalem and came to Bethphage, to the Mount of Olives, then Jesus sent two disciples, [2] saying to them, "Go into the village opposite you, and immediately you will find an ass tied, and a colt with her; untie them and bring them to me. [3] If any one says anything to you, you shall say, 'The Lord has need of them,' and he will send them immediately." [4] This took place to fulfil what was spoken by the prophet, saying, [5] "Tell the daughter of Zion, Behold, your king is coming to you, humble, and mounted on an ass, and on a colt, the foal of an ass." [6] The disciples went and did as Jesus had directed them; [7] they brought the ass and the colt, and put their garments on them, and he sat thereon. [8] Most of the crowd spread their garments on the road, and others cut branches from the trees and spread them on the road. [9] And the crowds that went before him and that followed him shouted, "Hosanna to the Son of David! Blessed is he who comes in the name of the Lord! Hosanna in the highest!" [10] And when he entered Jerusalem, all the city was stirred, saying, "Who is this?" [11] And the crowds said, "This is the prophet Jesus from Nazareth of Galilee."

Jesus did not enter Jerusalem on a horse as a great conquering king, but as a meek and humble servant, on an ass, the work beast of the poor. In doing so, he fulfilled the Old Testament description of the triumphant king: "Lo, your king comes to you . . . humble and riding on an ass" (Zechariah 9:9).

Though Jesus may not have met the expectation of some people for the Messiah, clearly there was something about him that moved people. When he entered Jerusalem, "all the city was stirred" (21:10). Perhaps it was because this great king came as one of them, not high on a horse above people, but lowly and without pomp and panoply.

Jesus is, as Peter confessed, the "Son of the living God" (Matthew 16:16). He is "Lord," but he does not "lord" it over us. He is one of us, living among us. Though he is the King of heaven and earth, the King of glory, he is still approachable. He came not to conquer or oppress, but to free us.

It is almost incomprehensible that in the incarnation, Christ—the Word of God—became human. Yet, not only did Christ "take the form of a servant" by becoming man, he also "humbled himself and became obedient unto death, even death on a cross" (Philippians 2:7,8). He could have come as a great earthly king, seated on a magnificent throne, the object of adoration. Instead, he identified with the lowly and poor. His only moment of glory on earth was this: Riding into Jerusalem on an ass. He would go to any lengths to draw us close to him, as Pope John Paul II observed in his book, *Crossing the Threshold of Hope:*

> Could God go further in his stooping down, in his drawing near to man, thereby expanding the possibilities of our knowing him? In truth, it seems that he has gone as far as possible. He could not go further. In a certain sense, God has gone too far! (page 40)

"Lord Jesus, thank you for becoming man. Not only did you lower yourself to become one of us, you chose to live on earth as a humble and meek servant so that we could come to you. Give us the grace to embrace this humility for ourselves."

Matthew 21:12-17

12 And Jesus entered the temple of God and drove out all who sold and bought in the temple, and he overturned the tables of the money-changers and the seats of those who sold pigeons. 13 He said to them, "It is written, 'My house shall be called a house of prayer'; but you make it a den of robbers."

14 And the blind and the lame came to him in the temple, and he healed them. 15 But when the chief priests and the scribes saw the wonderful things that he did, and the children crying out in the temple, "Hosanna to the Son of David!" they were indignant; 16 and they said to him, "Do you hear what these are saying?" And Jesus said to them, "Yes; have you never read, 'Out of the mouth of babes and sucklings thou hast brought perfect praise'?" 17 And leaving them, he went out of the city to Bethany and lodged there.

My house shall be called a house of prayer. (Matthew 21:13)

Jesus humbled himself and became man to turn the hearts of all people back to God. Jesus willingly accepted this mission because he longed for God to receive the thanks, praise, and worship of those he had created. With this in mind, we can better understand why Jesus became angry at what he saw happening in the temple.

When Jesus entered the temple, traders were selling the people the things used for sacrifices so that the priests could offer these gifts to God according to the law. In Jesus' time, sacrifices offered to God at the altar could be bought and sold. This practice, which was regulated by the temple authorities, was not what angered Jesus. Rather, it was the hardness of the people's hearts. They believed that this form of worship would satisfy God and fulfill their obligations. To God, however, these sacrifices had become empty worship.

A sacrifice pleasing to God is one which comes from "a broken and contrite heart" (Psalm 51:17). God does not want sacrifices where there is no true conversion of the heart. To him these are empty. Rather, he wants a people who "keep justice, and do righteousness," who keep "the sabbath, not profaning it." He seeks people who choose things that please him and who hold fast to the covenant (Isaiah 56:1-2,4; see also Jeremiah 7:1-15).

We are given the opportunity each day to offer worship pleasing to God. When we choose to do what we know God desires rather than what is self-serving, we are offering pleasing sacrifices. Whenever we choose generosity over self-centeredness or humility over pride, our lives are pleasing to God. Each day we must accept the truths we read in scripture about how we should live our lives. We need to do the same with what the Holy Spirit reveals to us in our prayer times and during our worship services. In this way, the temples of our bodies will become houses of prayer and we will offer sacrifices pleasing to God.

"Holy Spirit, source of all wisdom and knowledge, reveal the truth of Jesus to us. Help us to have a heart that loves God and wants to offer him thanks and praise as a pleasing sacrifice."

Matthew 21:18-22

[18] In the morning, as he was returning to the city, he was hungry. [19] And seeing a fig tree by the wayside he went to it, and found nothing on it but leaves only. And he said to it, "May no fruit ever come from you again!" And the fig tree withered at once. [20] When the disciples saw it they marveled, saying, "How did the fig tree wither at once?" [21] And Jesus answered them, "Truly, I say to you, if you have faith and never doubt, you will not only do what has been done to the fig tree, but even if you say to this mountain, 'Be taken up and cast into the sea,' it will be done. [22] And whatever you ask in prayer, you will receive, if you have faith."

J esus was hungry. Searching for a fig, he found none, and so he destroyed the tree because of its fruitlessness. The tree had failed to bear the fruit for which it had been created and nurtured.

Consider that we were created to know, love, and serve God. Do we see in our lives the "fruit" for which we were created? When we keep the Lord and our faith "boxed in"—separate from our everyday life and thoughts—then the fruit we bear will likely be for ourselves, not for our Savior. When the Lord is at the center of our lives and our hearts, however, we will naturally "bear fruit" for him. Everything we do will be directed toward his honor and glory.

Jesus told his disciples that if they "have faith and never doubt" (Matthew 21:21), they could do more than simply wither a fig tree; they could move mountains. According to the *Catechism of the Catholic Church*, "Faith is an entirely free gift that God makes to man." Yet we can lose this priceless gift. "To live, grow, and persevere in the faith until the end we must nourish it with the word of God; we must beg the Lord to increase our faith; it must be 'working through charity,' abounding in hope, and rooted in the faith of the Church" (CCC,162).

In our journey through this earthly life, we probably will have moments when we feel weak in our faith. When we have moments of doubt, we should ask our Father to strengthen our faith. "Whatever you ask in prayer, you will receive, if you have faith," Jesus promised (Matthew 21:22).

Jesus used this incident to teach his disciples about faith, but his action can also be viewed prophetically. The miracle prefigured the eventual destruction of the temple and the fall of Jerusalem in 70 A.D., when the Holy City was cleared of all those who failed to bear the fruit of righteousness for the Lord. Faith is the soil and nourishment that will allow our lives to become fruitful. If we fail to nurture our faith, we, too, will have little fruit to bear for the Lord.

"Father in heaven, we come to you in complete confidence. Grant our petition to increase our faith. Banish all our doubts, and give us the faith that will move mountains. Allow our faith to be a witness to others and to be the soil that brings forth the fruit in our lives."

Matthew 21:23-27

^{23} And when he entered the temple, the chief priests and the elders of the people came up to him as he was teaching, and said, "By what authority are you doing these things, and who gave you this authority?" ^{24} Jesus answered them, "I also will ask you a question; and if you tell me the answer, then I also will tell you by what authority I do these things. ^{25} The baptism of John, whence was it? From heaven or from men?" And they argued with one another, "If we say, 'From heaven,' he will say to us, 'Why then did you not believe him?' ^{26} But if we say, 'From men,' we are afraid of the multitude; for all hold that John was a prophet." ^{27} So they answered Jesus, "We do not know." And he said to them, "Neither will I tell you by what authority I do these things."

Two of the most important concepts in this passage are those of "authority" (Matthew 21:23) and "from heaven" (21:25). Both lead the reader to consider the nature of Jesus as divine (from heaven) and as having received his authority to act from the Father, who is in heaven. These concepts help us better understand who Jesus is and what our daily response to him should be.

All of Jesus' authority came from the Father. It was not of human origin; it was from heaven. Before time began, before creation, Jesus as the Word was present with the Father (John 1:1). Everything that was created was created through him (John 1:3; Colossians 1:16).

In his resurrection, Jesus was given as man authority over all that was created. In his own words: "All authority in heaven and on earth has been given to me" (Matthew 28:18). With what reverence and awe should we come into Jesus' presence and acknowledge his holiness! We should tremble at the thought of approaching such holiness. And yet this holy God has chosen to draw near to us. "I dwell in the high and holy place, and also with him who is of a contrite and humble spirit, to revive the spirit of the humble, and to revive the heart of the contrite" (Isaiah 57:15).

The Father sent his Son to dwell among us. In an Advent address, Pope John Paul II spoke of the nearness of God to us through his Son:

> God has given the greatest testimony of his nearness by sending on earth his Word, the second person of the Most Holy Trinity, who took on a body like ours and came to live among us.

The Pope also pointed out what our response should be when he added:

> With gratitude for this condescension of God who desired to draw near to us . . . by addressing us in the very person of his only begotten Son, we repeat with humble and joyous faith: "You alone are the Holy One, you alone are the Lord, you alone are the Most High, Jesus Christ, with the Holy Spirit, in the glory of God the Father, Amen."

Let us draw near to this God, who has drawn near to us. In faith and trust, let us accept his authority over our lives and pray that his kingdom would extend over every nation and race.

Matthew 21:28-32

[28] "What do you think? A man had two sons; and he went to the first and said, 'Son, go and work in the vineyard today.' [29] And he answered, 'I will not'; but afterward he repented and went. [30] And he went to the second and said the same; and he answered, 'I go, sir,' but did not go. [31] Which of the two did the will of his father?" They said, "The first." Jesus said to them, "Truly, I say to you, the tax collectors and the harlots go into the kingdom of God before you. [32] For John came to you in the way of righteousness, and you did not believe him, but the tax collectors and the harlots believed him; and even when you saw it, you did not afterward repent and believe him."

How many times have you quickly agreed to do something and then failed to follow through? Or refused to do something only to rethink your position later and complete the job? Both instant willingness without follow-through and reluctant accountability can show weakness, a lack of love, and imprecision of purpose.

Combine the quick "yes" of the second son with the ultimate commitment of the first, and we see a snapshot of Jesus. He always sought the will of the Father, looked to God for the power to obey, and faithfully accomplished God's will. Before creation, Jesus agreed to become man for our salvation. As God incarnate, he was perfected through suffering as he constantly sought to please his Father. It was through this obedience that he won for us salvation and reconciliation with God. Jesus never weighed the Father's will against his own as we so often do. He was tempted and he suffered, but he "did not count equality with God a thing to be grasped";

rather he "emptied himself, taking the form of a servant. . . . And being found in human form he humbled himself and became obedient unto death, even death on a cross" (Philippians 2:6,8).

Through his cross, Jesus paved the way for us to be obedient to the Father as well. We have but to receive the grace that is our inheritance as children of God. This is the reason he created us; we need not shrink back from difficult situations, but only look to Christ. In every situation, God only asks that we do our best without fear of failure or of what we might be losing. And, when we fall short, he graciously calls us to repent and be strengthened.

God our Father deeply desires to help us. Knowing our weaknesses, he continually invites us to turn to him. "When a wicked man turns away from the wickedness he has committed and does what is lawful and right, he shall save his life" (Ezekiel 18:27).

In the Eucharist, we worship and honor Jesus; we ask for his mercy and receive his strength. Jesus paid a high price for us, agreeing to do the Father's will and perfectly carrying it out despite the suffering. So great was his love for us that he held back nothing in rescuing us from sin. We have only to be open to him to receive the precious gift of his love. In Jesus' body and blood we have the guarantee of all that we seek and desire.

Matthew 21:33-46

[33] "Hear another parable. There was a householder who planted a vineyard, and set a hedge around it, and dug a wine press in it, and built a tower, and let it out to tenants, and went into another country. [34] When the season of fruit drew near, he sent his servants to the tenants, to get his fruit; [35] and the tenants took his servants and beat one, killed another, and stoned another. [36] Again he sent other servants, more than the first; and they did the same to them. [37] Afterward he sent his son to them, saying, 'They will respect my son.' [38] But when the tenants saw the son, they said to themselves, 'This is the heir; come, let us kill him and have his inheritance.' [39] And they took him and cast him out of the vineyard, and killed him. [40] When therefore the owner of the vineyard comes, what will he do to those tenants?" [41] They said to him, "He will put those wretches to a miserable death, and let out the vineyard to other tenants who will give him the fruits in their seasons."

[42] Jesus said to them, "Have you never read in the scriptures: 'The very stone which the builders rejected has become the head of the corner; this was the Lord's doing, and it is marvelous in our eyes'? [43] Therefore I tell you, the kingdom of God will be taken away from you and given to a nation producing the fruits of it. [44] And he who falls on this stone will be broken to pieces; but when it falls on any one, it will crush him."

[45] When the chief priests and the Pharisees heard his parables, they perceived that he was speaking about them. [46] But when they tried to arrest him, they feared the multitudes, because they held him to be a prophet.

Jesus' depiction of the Jewish nation as God's vineyard would have been a familiar concept to his listeners. The details were similar to those of Isaiah's parable of the house of Israel, the vineyard of the Lord, set apart and cherished by God for his particular favor (Isaiah 5:1-7).

The story of the wicked tenants is an allegory of salvation history. God, the owner of the vineyard, left his people in the care and protection of religious and political leaders. Their responsibility was to bring the people to fruitfulness in knowing, loving, and obeying God so they might continue to enjoy his love and protection. From time to time God sent his prophets to remind the people of this purpose, but the prophets were abused, rejected, and even murdered. Finally, God sent his Son, but he too was reviled and put to death.

Jesus' mission on earth was to form the church, a new people of God. United by submission and obedience to the Father's will, they would live out the fullness of God's life and love, and would one day enjoy the eternal inheritance promised to all the faithful. We are often like the tenants who sought by devious means to obtain the owner's inheritance (Matthew 21:38), and thus become our own lord and master. There is a pride in the human heart that spurs us to take control of our lives and find fulfillment apart from God and obedience to him.

God's earnest desire is that the members of his church listen to and commit their lives to his Son as they hear God's word in prayer, scripture, and celebration of the liturgy. It is only through Jesus and in union with him that we can recognize the voice of the Holy Spirit. As we hear his voice and turn to God, we will "have no anxiety about anything" and our minds will be raised to heavenly realities, enabling us to think about whatever is true, honorable, just, pure, lovely, and gracious (Philippians 4:6,8).

Thank God in prayer for the love he offers you in Jesus and for the intimacy to which he calls you as a member of his church. Ask Jesus to be the Lord of your life so that—living in him and for him—you may be faithful to God, know the peace and glory of his favor and protection, and return to him the fruit that is his due (Matthew 21:34).

Matthew 22:1-14

[1] And again Jesus spoke to them in parables, saying, [2] "The kingdom of heaven may be compared to a king who gave a marriage feast for his son, [3] and sent his servants to call those who were invited to the marriage feast; but they would not come. [4] Again he sent other servants, saying, 'Tell those who are invited, Behold, I have made ready my dinner, my oxen and my fat calves are killed, and everything is ready; come to the marriage feast.' [5] But they made light of it and went off, one to his farm, another to his business, [6] while the rest seized his servants, treated them shamefully, and killed them. [7] The king was angry, and he sent his troops and destroyed those murderers and burned their city. [8] Then he said to his servants, 'The wedding is ready, but those invited were not worthy. [9] Go therefore to the thoroughfares, and invite to the marriage feast as many as you find.' [10] And those servants went out into the streets and gathered all whom they found, both bad and good; so the wedding hall was filled with guests.
[11] "But when the king came in to look at the guests, he saw there a man who had no wedding garment; [12] and he said to him, 'Friend, how did you get in here without a wedding garment?' And he was speechless. [13] Then the king said to the attendants, 'Bind him hand and foot, and cast him into the outer darkness; there

men will weep and gnash their teeth.' [14] For many are called, but few are chosen." ▨▨

In his abundant mercy, God invites all people to the royal banquet for the wedding of his Son to the church. The prophet Isaiah announced the Lord's invitation: "On this mountain the LORD of hosts will make for all peoples a feast" (Isaiah 25:6). In the parable of the wedding feast, we again read of a banquet open to all people, a feast from which no one is excluded (Matthew 22:1-14).

Isaiah and Jesus both emphasized that the Lord's invitation was not an exclusive, high-society event. All are invited regardless of state in life, position in the community, material wealth, race, age, or handicap. The mixing of social groups was just as radical a concept in Isaiah's and Jesus' time as it is in ours. The Pharisees of Jesus' day, for instance, shunned tax collectors and sinners—but these "sinners" often accepted Jesus before the self-righteous Pharisees did (Matthew 9:10-12). Today, the educated and financially secure often shun the gospel, while the poor and humble embrace it eagerly.

In the sacrament of the Eucharist, God invites all people to taste his great love. As we participate in the liturgy of the Eucharist, God increases our desire and readiness for the heavenly banquet that is to come. How will we respond to the Lord's invitation to the wedding banquet of his Son? Will we be too preoccupied with worldly affairs to accept it humbly? Or will we respond with hearts overflowing with love and gratitude for the Lord's gift of refreshment and the opportunity to dwell in his house for ever (Psalm 23:3,6)?

Jesus said: "Many are called, but few are chosen" (Matthew 22:14). The king rejected the improperly dressed man because he did not regard his invitation as a great honor. Consequently, he did not bother to clothe himself with "the new nature, created after the likeness of God in true righteousness and holiness" (Ephesians 4:24). The guests who were dressed in wedding garments recognized God's abundant mercy and love as their only source of strength and hope, and so they "clothed" themselves with this mercy.

Let us embrace God's gift of love and grace in the Eucharist. By so doing, he will enable us to accept wholeheartedly his invitation to join in the celebration of the wedding of the Lamb.

Matthew 22:15-22

[15] Then the Pharisees went and took counsel how to entangle him in his talk. [16] And they sent their disciples to him, along with the Herodians, saying, "Teacher, we know that you are true, and teach the way of God truthfully, and care for no man; for you do not regard the position of men. [17] Tell us, then, what you think. Is it lawful to pay taxes to Caesar, or not?" [18] But Jesus, aware of their malice, said, "Why put me to the test, you hypocrites? [19] Show me the money for the tax." And they brought him a coin. [20] And Jesus said to them, "Whose likeness and inscription is this?" [21] They said, "Caesar's." Then he said to them, "Render therefore to Caesar the things that are Caesar's, and to God the things that are God's." [22] When they heard it, they marveled; and they left him and went away.

The motivation of the Pharisees and the Herodians in questioning Jesus about the legality of paying taxes to Caesar was quickly exposed by Jesus' response: "Render therefore to Caesar the things that are the Caesar's, and to God the things that are God's" (Matthew 22:21). As citizens of the empire, they owed the emperor allegiance but, first and foremost, they owed God allegiance, for "there is no authority except from God" (Romans 13:1).

As adopted children of our heavenly Father, we are citizens of a heavenly kingdom. We are called and chosen to be a holy people, set apart for God's praise and glory (Ephesians 1:4-6). The Father wants us to share his divine life now as well as in eternity, to develop an intimacy of relationship with him, speaking with him in prayer and hearing from him through his word. We are gifted with the high dignity of being made in God's image and likeness (Genesis 1:27). We have received a privileged citizenship and, with it, a call to extend God's kingdom on earth.

This is why, even as a people set apart, we need to see the importance of public affairs. The Fathers of the Second Vatican Council taught: "The Church regards as worthy of praise and consideration the work of those who, as a service to others, dedicate themselves to the welfare of the state and undertake the burdens of this task" (On the Church in the Modern World, 75). Followers of Christ are called to bring an authentic Christian voice to governmental and political affairs.

The Christian life is not set in opposition to civil life. As a result of our first parents' decision to usurp God's authority (Genesis 3:1-19), obedience to authority, whatever its nature, goes against our desire for independence. Even so, Jesus died that all people might acknowledge God's authority in their lives. By appropriating his power and that of his cross, the desires of our fallen nature can be overcome; by our witness of obedience, God's kingdom can come and reign among us. God's plan for our lives far exceeds our imaginings. His plan includes obedience to the laws of governing authorities—and God's plan will not be thwarted. The prophet Isaiah recognized Cyrus of Persia as God's instrument for fulfilling his plan for the Jews to be returned from exile in Babylon to restore Jerusalem and its temple (Isaiah 45:1,4-6). Let us pray that our minds be penetrated by the light of the Holy Spirit so that we may recognize and respond to God's plan for us.

Matthew 22:23-33

23 The same day Sadducees came to him, who say that there is no resurrection; and they asked him a question, 24 saying, "Teacher, Moses said, 'If a man dies, having no children, his brother must marry the widow, and raise up children for his brother.' 25 Now there were seven brothers among us; the first married, and died, and having no children left his wife to his brother. 26 So too the second and third, down to the seventh. 27 After them all, the woman died. 28 In the resurrection, therefore, to which of the seven will she be wife? For they all had her."

29 But Jesus answered them, "You are wrong, because you know neither the scriptures nor the power of God. 30 For in the resurrection they neither marry nor are given in marriage, but are like angels in heaven. 31 And as for the resurrection of the dead, have you not read what was said to you by God, 32 'I am the God of Abraham, and the God of Isaac, and the God of Jacob'? He is not God of the dead, but of the living." 33 And when the crowd heard it, they were astonished at his teaching.

The Sadducees did not believe in the resurrection of the body after death. Thus, their intent was devious when they asked Jesus about the oft-married widow of seven brothers (Matthew 22:28). Their hope was to trap Jesus in his words. Jesus seized the opportunity to teach about the truth and nature of the resurrection. He explained that when a person rises to eternal life the laws of our earthly life no longer apply. All become like angels in heaven; all are satisfied with the glory of God. He admonished them for knowing neither the scriptures nor the power of God (22:29).

Jesus taught that hope in the resurrection is based on the character of God. God is a living spirit who is faithful to his promises (Psalm 145:13). He is all-present, eternal, and continually offering us life (John 10:10; 1 John 5:11). The promise of salvation is a promise of eternal life with God. The Sadducees were missing the message of the book of Moses (Exodus 3:6) pointing to the truth that God is the God of the living, not of the dead.

What about us? Do we believe in resurrection? Is that the goal for which we are striving? In order for the resurrection to be a living truth giving us hope, we, too, must know the scriptures and the power of God. This is what affirms in our hearts the truth of the resurrection. If we favor the truth of this world and ignore the truth of scripture and the testimony of God's power, our hearts will not be open to allow the Spirit to teach us the ways of God. If we do not know the power of God giving witness to scripture, God's power to do all that he has promised will never be affirmed in our lives.

St. Paul wrote: "If the Spirit of him who raised Jesus from the dead dwells in you, he who raised Christ Jesus from the dead will give life to your mortal bodies also through his Spirit who dwells in you" (Romans 8:11). The fullness of the resurrection will only be known to us after we join Jesus in heaven, but we can—through faith, enlightened by the Holy Spirit—live with a growing expectation of the hope that is ours in Christ Jesus.

Let us pray with Paul: "That I may know him and the power of his resurrection, and may share his sufferings, becoming like him in death, that if possible I may attain the resurrection from the dead" (Philippians 3:10-11).

Matthew 22:34-40

34 But when the Pharisees heard that he had silenced the Sadducees, they came together. 35 And one of them, a lawyer, asked him a question, to test him. 36 "Teacher, which is the great commandment in the law?" 37 And he said to him, "You shall love the Lord your God with all your heart, and with all your soul, and with all your mind. 38 This is the great and first commandment. 39 And a second is like it, You shall love your neighbor as yourself. 40 On these two commandments depend all the law and the prophets."

In asking which is the greatest commandment, the Pharisees expected Jesus to tell them what he felt was most essential about the law. Jesus' answer—love of God and neighbor—centers all observance of the law on love. To those who heard him, people whose whole culture and way of life was based on the law, Jesus was saying that every detail of their lives depended on love.

St. Paul understood this. "Love is the fulfilling of the law" (Romans 13:10). It draws our souls willingly to God. The Father demonstrated love by sending his only Son to bring us forgiveness and to reconcile us to the Father. Jesus, who is God's "love calling us to love in return" (Abbot William of St. Thierry, *The Contemplation of God*), lived it by saying "yes" to the Father's plan, even though it meant leaving the throne of heaven and dying on the cross at the hands of the people he had created. We experience that love when we unite ourselves to God's will.

The world has saturated our thoughts about love with human ideology. We are steeped in popular notions absorbed from television, movies, magazines, and books of all kinds. We tend to think of love as emotional, sensual, uncontrollable; we *fall* in love as if we stumbled over it in the dark, or wake up to find that love has gone as if it were a coward that had fled at daylight. But we are called to will and to do what God wants and are empowered to do this by his love for us. That, and not a feeling inside, is love of God.

Love of God means that we worship him only, not our families, jobs, or possessions; loving our neighbors means that we are patient, kind, and "bear all things" (1 Corinthians 13:4,7). To understand this, we must first ask God to teach us what his love is, to teach us what these injunctions mean in our lives. Only if our love is rooted in the love of God will it bear fruit for the salvation of others. We love God when we choose his will and obey it. The power comes from God—the decision is ours. Let us open ourselves and ask him to teach us. Then we will be able to love our neighbor as God loves—freely, generously, and without reservation.

Matthew 22:41-46

[41] Now while the Pharisees were gathered together, Jesus asked them a question, [42] saying, "What do you think of the Christ? Whose son is he?" They said to him, "The son of David." [43] He said to them, "How is it then that David, inspired by the Spirit, calls him Lord, saying, [44] 'The Lord said to my Lord, Sit at my right hand, till I put your enemies under your feet'? [45] If David thus calls him Lord, how is he his son?" [46] And no one was able to answer him a word, nor from that day did any one dare to ask him any more questions.

Jesus was teaching and preaching in the temple courts when the chief priests, elders, and teachers of the law challenged his authority to do so. Jesus responded with questions which could help them to raise their minds above the earthly level, which was so often political or legal in nature. The scribes and teachers had a political and nationalistic concept of the mission of the awaited Messiah.

The Davidic sonship of the Messiah was firmly grounded in Hebrew scripture (Psalm 110:1; Isaiah 9:2-7; 2 Samuel 7:11-14). Jesus' challenge was intended to help the people see the full truth as it is revealed in the scriptures. The Holy Spirit had revealed to David that the Messiah was not only the "son of David" but his Lord. Jesus was trying to help people to see that the work of the Messiah was not simply to extend the dynasty of David, but to establish a kingdom, the throne of which would be at the right hand of God.

How are we to know the truth that Jesus teaches, indeed that Jesus is God, that the Holy Spirit exists, that Christ established the church, that there *is* a God? Let us ask the Holy Spirit to teach us the truth of these things, especially who Jesus is as Lord and Savior. "The Holy Spirit, whom the Father will send in my name, he will teach you all things, and bring to your remembrance all that I have said to you" (John 14:26).

As we pray and study scripture, the Holy Spirit can inspire us with knowledge and revelation. Have faith and believe the truths that the church proclaims at the heart of her faith. With this as the starting point, the Spirit can help us to understand with our spirits as well as our minds. St. Augustine said: "I do not seek to understand in order to believe; I believe in order to understand." In these days of uncertainty, we need the Spirit to teach us so that we will be able to stand firm in our faith, no matter what. As we stand firm, we will come to understand by the work of the Spirit.

"Heavenly Father, through the Spirit, enlighten us to know the mystery of your plan for your people. Give us the faith to believe and the enlightenment to understand."

Matthew 23:1-12

[1] Then said Jesus to the crowds and to his disciples, [2] "The scribes and the Pharisees sit on Moses' seat; [3] so practice and observe whatever they tell you, but not what they do; for they preach, but do not practice. [4] They bind heavy burdens, hard to bear, and lay them on men's shoulders; but they themselves will not move them with their finger. [5] They do all their deeds to be seen by men; for they make their phylacteries broad and their fringes long, [6] and they love the place of honor at feasts and the best seats in the synagogues, [7] and salutations in the market places, and being called rabbi by men. [8] But you are not to be called rabbi, for you have one teacher, and you are all brethren. [9] And call no man your father on earth, for you have one Father, who is in heaven. [10] Neither be called masters, for you have one master, the Christ. [11] He who is greatest among you shall be your servant; [12] whoever exalts himself will be humbled, and whoever humbles himself will be exalted."

The scribes and Pharisees were doing God's work in their preaching and teaching, but in doing so, they were trying to draw attention to themselves. "They do all their deeds to be seen by men" (Matthew 23:5). They sought the place of honor at feasts, the best seats in the synagogues, and reverent titles. They were victims of their own pride and vanity. They had forgotten whom they were serving.

It is natural for us to want to draw attention to ourselves. Perhaps because of our fallen nature, we enjoy being at the center of things, especially when what we do has a laudable purpose. We like to feel important, valued, and appreciated.

Jesus' words remind us that even when we are doing his work, we must be careful that we serve by washing the feet of others—not by asking others to wash our feet. The "greatest"—those in positions that involve leadership and visibility—must possess the largest heart, a servant's heart. Their motivation for serving must be love for others, not to bring glory to themselves.

Although contrary to our baser instincts, what we need is a willingness to forget ourselves. Our purest moments of love are those in which we let go of our vision of ourselves and focus on the needs of others. It is this disposition of self-abandonment that draws us closer to the Lord, as we are caught up in his love and goodness. When we serve others, letting go of our need to feel important or valued, we imitate our Lord Jesus. He who was truly the greatest among us was also a servant who washed the feet of his disciples.

When we find ourselves consumed by prideful attitudes, we need to repent and ask the Lord to help us serve as he served. The more we become aware of our prideful tendencies, the more we can rise above them, with God's grace.

"Lord Jesus, help us to be like you. You served us out of love and never out of a desire to be honored. Take away our pride and fill us with your humility. Give us the grace to love others and to forget ourselves."

Matthew 23:13-36

[13] "But woe to you, scribes and Pharisees, hypocrites! because you shut the kingdom of heaven against men; for you neither enter yourselves, nor allow those who would enter to go in. [14] Woe to you, scribes and Pharisees, hypocrites! for you traverse sea and land to make a single proselyte, and when he becomes a proselyte, you make him twice as much a child of hell as yourselves.

[16] "Woe to you, blind guides, who say, 'If any one swears by the temple, it is nothing; but if any one swears by the gold of the temple, he is bound by his oath.' [17] You blind fools! For which is greater, the gold or the temple that has made the gold sacred? [18] And you say, 'If any one swears by the altar, it is nothing; but if any one swears by the gift that is on the altar, he is bound by his oath.' [19] You blind men! For which is greater, the gift or the altar that makes the gift sacred? [20] So he who swears by the altar, swears by it and by everything on it; [21] and he who swears by the temple, swears by it and by him who dwells in it; [22] and he who swears by heaven, swears by the throne of God and by him who sits upon it.

[23] "Woe to you, scribes and Pharisees, hypocrites! for you tithe mint and dill and cummin, and have neglected the weightier matters of the law, justice and mercy and faith; these you ought to have done, without neglecting the others. [24] You blind guides, straining out a gnat and swallowing a camel!

[25] "Woe to you, scribes and Pharisees, hypocrites! for you cleanse the outside of the cup and of the plate, but inside they are full of extortion and rapacity. [26] You blind Pharisee! first cleanse the inside of the cup and of the plate, that the outside also may be clean.

[27] "Woe to you, scribes and Pharisees, hypocrites! for you are like whitewashed tombs, which outwardly appear beautiful, but within they are full of dead men's bones and all uncleanness. [28] So you also outwardly appear righteous to men, but within you are full of

hypocrisy and iniquity.

29 "Woe to you, scribes and Pharisees, hypocrites! for you build the tombs of the prophets and adorn the monuments of the righteous, 30 saying, 'If we had lived in the days of our fathers, we would not have taken part with them in shedding the blood of the prophets.' 31 Thus you witness against yourselves, that you are sons of those who murdered the prophets. 32 Fill up, then, the measure of your fathers.

33 You serpents, you brood of vipers, how are you to escape being sentenced to hell? 34 Therefore I send you prophets and wise men and scribes, some of whom you will kill and crucify, and some you will scourge in your synagogues and persecute from town to town, 35 that upon you may come all the righteous blood shed on earth, from the blood of innocent Abel to the blood of Zechariah the son of Barachiah, whom you murdered between the sanctuary and the altar. 36 Truly, I say to you, all this will come upon this generation".

W hy would Jesus choose to rebuke the scribes and Pharisees, those who were religious leaders of his day? Despite the power they wielded, Jesus minced no words when addressing the state of their religious practices. His grief at their state moved him to pronounce these woes, giving them a clear warning of the unhappy consequences of their behavior. He recognized that they were using religion for their own purposes, exalting themselves and rejecting true faith. He was compelled to confront their sin which—if left unchecked—would lead them to spiritual death.

In the first two "woes," Jesus accused the scribes and Pharisees of hindering people from truly entering into the kingdom of God (Matthew 23:13,15). Not only did the religious leaders choose not to enter, they blocked the way for others by their rejection of Christ. He pointed to their hypocrisy in claiming to lead people to God, but failing to encourage true holiness. Instead, they had set up an aura of religiosity, and the people were worse off than ever. Finally, Jesus called the Pharisees and scribes "blind guides" because they were missing the essence of the truth regarding oath-taking (23:16). They had become blind to the true worth of God's presence among them. This woe echoed Jesus' statement from the beatitudes forbidding the making of oaths and encouraging his followers to live honest and pure lives (5:33-37).

These woes are modeled on Isaiah (5:8-23), who declared the ruin of those who, through greed and falsehood, distorted true justice and righteousness. In the gospel, Jesus portrayed the Pharisees and scribes as those who had exchanged the truth of God for human ideas about religion. Matthew used this passage to warn the early Christian community against similar tendencies among them. We too can take these words as a warning in light of our own situations. Let us ask the Holy Spirit, the Spirit of truth, to show us how we may have distorted the gospel to meet our own ends.

"Holy Spirit, open our eyes to any ways in which we use religion for our own purposes. Forgive us for our actions that try to manipulate the word of God instead of allowing it to pierce us and bring us to holiness."

Matthew 23:37-39

[37] "O Jerusalem, Jerusalem, killing the prophets and stoning those who are sent to you! How often would I have gathered your children together as a hen gathers her brood under her wings, and you would not! [38] Behold, your house is forsaken and desolate. [39] For I tell you, you will not see me again, until you say, 'Blessed is he who comes in the name of the Lord.' " ▨▨▨▨

In the gospels, Jesus spoke very clearly many times of his immi-
nent death. Matthew reported several occasions when Jesus, still far from Jerusalem, prophesied his coming passion, death and resurrection (See Matthew 16:21; 17:22-23; 20:17-19).

Jesus was willing to accept death because he understood God's plan of redemption and wanted to be obedient to the Father in all things. God saw that his people had turned away from his love and, as a result, had fallen into every kind of sin. Jesus knew that because his people had refused to be gathered together in him, they would end up desolate, separated from the Father's love and protection.

Jesus chose to become man in order to take upon himself the punishment that our sins deserved. He realized that the road to Jerusalem and the ascent to Calvary were part of his mission. He knew that his work of reconciling sinners to God would only be accomplished through his death and resurrection. Jesus loved us too much to shrink back from his calling. Even though he was quite aware that Jerusalem had been the death of many a prophet before him (Matthew 23:37), he was determined to destroy sin so he could finally gather his people in his arms.

Jesus' work of healing and miracles was important, but his atoning sacrifice was the only way in which God's plan to save humanity could be fulfilled. By the blood shed on the cross, God's wrath against sinners was removed. Jesus did not just endure the cross; he chose it freely as the Father's plan for him. He embraced it out of love, moving forward steadily toward Jerusalem because it meant life for God's people. Filled with gratitude for Jesus' sacrifice and love, let us cry out in one voice: "Blessed is he who comes in the name of the Lord!"

A DEVOTIONAL COMMENTARY ON MATTHEW

The End of the Age

MATTHEW
24–25

Matthew 24:1-35

1   Jesus left the temple and was going away, when his disciples came to point out to him the buildings of the temple. 2 But he answered them, "You see all these, do you not? Truly, I say to you, there will not be left here one stone upon another, that will not be thrown down."

3   As he sat on the Mount of Olives, the disciples came to him privately, saying, "Tell us, when will this be, and what will be the sign of your coming and of the close of the age?" 4 And Jesus answered them, "Take heed that no one leads you astray. 5 For many will come in my name, saying, 'I am the Christ,' and they will lead many astray. 6 And you will hear of wars and rumors of wars; see that you are not alarmed; for this must take place, but the end is not yet. 7 For nation will rise against nation, and kingdom against kingdom, and there will be famines and earthquakes in various places: 8 all this is but the beginning of the birth-pangs.

9   "Then they will deliver you up to tribulation, and put you to death; and you will be hated by all nations for my name's sake. 10 And then many will fall away, and betray one another, and hate one another. 11 And many false prophets will arise and lead many astray. 12 And because wickedness is multiplied, most men's love will grow cold. 13 But he who endures to the end will be saved. 14 And this gospel of the kingdom will be preached throughout the whole world, as a testimony to all nations; and then the end will come.

15   "So when you see the desolating sacrilege spoken of by the prophet Daniel, standing in the holy place (let the reader understand), 16 then let those who are in Judea flee to the mountains; 17 let him who is on the housetop not go down to take what is in his house; 18 and let him who is in the field not turn back to take his mantle. 19 And alas for those who are with child and for those who give suck in those days! 20 Pray that your flight may not

be in winter or on a sabbath. [21] For then there will be great
tribulation, such as has not been from the beginning of the world
until now, no, and never will be. [22] And if those days had not been
shortened, no human being would be saved; but for the sake of the
elect those days will be shortened. [23] Then if any one says to you,
'Lo, here is the Christ!' or 'There he is!' do not believe it. [24] For
false Christs and false prophets will arise and show great signs and
wonders, so as to lead astray, if possible, even the elect. [25] Lo, I have
told you beforehand. [26] So, if they say to you, 'Lo, he is in the
wilderness,' do not go out; if they say, 'Lo, he is in the inner rooms,'
do not believe it. [27] For as the lightning comes from the east and
shines as far as the west, so will be the coming of the Son of man. [28]
Wherever the body is, there the eagles will be gathered together.
[29] "Immediately after the tribulation of those days the sun will be
darkened, and the moon will not give its light, and the stars will
fall from heaven, and the powers of the heavens will be shaken; [30]
then will appear the sign of the Son of man in heaven, and then all
the tribes of the earth will mourn, and they will see the Son of man
coming on the clouds of heaven with power and great glory; [31] and
he will send out his angels with a loud trumpet call, and they will
gather his elect from the four winds, from one end of heaven to the
other.
[32] "From the fig tree learn its lesson: as soon as its branch
becomes tender and puts forth its leaves, you know that summer is
near. [33] So also, when you see all these things, you know that he is
near, at the very gates. [34] Truly, I say to you, this generation will not
pass away till all these things take place. [35] Heaven and earth will
pass away, but my words will not pass away."

People of every age have pondered the burning question: "When will the end come? What will be the signs?" Theories and predictions have been many and varied. During the Old Testament period, prophets foretold the coming of the "day of the Lord," when humanity would witness the triumph of God over his enemies. The disciples of Jesus were as curious as we are about the end of the world, especially when they heard Jesus predict the destruction of the temple in Jerusalem (Matthew 24:2), which actually occurred in 70 A.D.

It is true that one day Jesus will return (Matthew 24:30; Acts 1:11). He will return as the Son of man, unmistakable and visible to all. His coming will be sudden and unexpected (1 Thessalonians 5:2-3) and will usher in a new heaven and a new earth. A series of disorders will portend the final days, including the appearance of impostors, times of political upheaval, and the occurrence of natural disasters (Matthew 24:6-13). Yet Jesus said not to be perturbed by these signs; the end will not come until there first has been a time of witnessing and persecution of the church (Luke 21:12-19).

Even if we believe that Jesus' coming is imminent, we do not know exactly *when* it will occur. "But of that day and hour no one knows, . . . but the Father only" (Matthew 24:36). The important thing for each of us is to live as if the Lord were coming today. Very simply, if we are watchful and diligent in our faith, we will be ready.

Each day that the Lord gives us, we should anticipate the coming of Christ. As we go about our daily tasks, even the most mundane ones, we can be looking forward to the joy that will be ours when Jesus comes to take us home. If we remain faithful to the Lord each day, we need not fear his coming: We are his. Our faith must rest in the promise of eternal life which was made to those who believe in him. No matter what circumstance we find ourselves in, we can unite our hearts with our brothers and sisters in the body of Christ and say, "Come, Lord Jesus."

Matthew 24:36-44

[36] "But of that day and hour no one knows, not even the angels of heaven, nor the Son, but the Father only. [37] As were the days of Noah, so will be the coming of the Son of man. [38] For as in those days before the flood they were eating and drinking, marrying and giving in marriage, until the day when Noah entered the ark, [39] and they did not know until the flood came and swept them all away, so will be the coming of the Son of man. [40] Then two men will be in the field; one is taken and one is left. [41] Two women will be grinding at the mill; one is taken and one is left.

[42] Watch therefore, for you do not know on what day your Lord is coming. [43] But know this, that if the householder had known in what part of the night the thief was coming, he would have watched and would not have let his house be broken into. [44] Therefore you also must be ready; for the Son of man is coming at an hour you do not expect."

*I was glad when they said to me, "Let us go to the house
of the LORD!" (Psalm 122:1)*

The psalmist proclaimed his joy as he joined the throngs of worshippers making their way toward the temple in Jerusalem. How much more should we rejoice in the knowledge that our Lord is coming to unite us to himself! "For salvation is nearer to us now than when we first believed" (Romans 13:11).

We may be somewhat puzzled by Jesus' words about his return: "Two men will be in the field; one is taken and one is left. . . . Watch therefore, for you do not know on what day your Lord is coming" (Matthew 24:40,42). This somewhat ominous prophecy seems almost contradictory to the psalmist's sense of joy.

The prophet Isaiah provided an insight on how these disparate themes of judgment and joy are to be reconciled. Inspired by the Holy Spirit, Isaiah foresaw the day when "many peoples shall come" to God's holy city "that he may teach us his ways and that we may walk in his paths" (Isaiah 2:3). The result of this divine intervention will be a profound peace, such as the world has never known: "Nation shall not lift up sword against nation, neither shall they learn war any more"(2:4). Jesus inaugurated what was prophesied; we have a foretaste of the promise now, but will know it in its fullness when Jesus comes again in glory.

We can prepare our hearts in anticipation of a closer union with God, both now and in the future. We make ready the way of the Lord, not out of fear, but because, in the deepest part of our being, we long to "walk in the light of the LORD" (Isaiah 2:5).

Jesus personally experienced this great longing in his human heart. He yearned for all men and women to share his unity with the Father and the Spirit. Thus, he warned us of the necessary judgment: "Be ready, for the Son of man is coming at an hour you do not expect" (Matthew 24:44). We prepare now in joy, for the day is approaching when our preparations and labor will be over. Like the psalmist, we, too, will sing for joy as we wait to meet our God.

Matthew 24:45-51

45 "Who then is the faithful and wise servant, whom his master has set over his household, to give them their food at the proper time? 46 Blessed is that servant whom his master when he comes will find so doing. 47 Truly, I say to you, he will set him over all his possessions. 48 But if that wicked servant says to himself, 'My master is delayed,' 49 and begins to beat his fellow servants, and eats and drinks with the drunken, 50 the master of that servant will come on a day when he does not expect him and at an hour he does not know, 51 and will punish him, and put him with the hypocrites; there men will weep and gnash their teeth."

Jesus' discourse concerning the end times challenges us to be prepared for the coming of the Son of man. To ignore his warning and live a life of self-centered pleasure-seeking would be unwise. The message here is reminiscent of the challenge expressed earlier (Matthew 7:24-26), when Jesus reminded his hearers that those who did not build their house on the rock of his words would see it fall. Thus, both at the beginning of his public ministry and as it drew to a close, Jesus put forth the same challenge and the same warning.

Such words of caution are not restricted to the New Testament; they occur throughout the Old Testament as well (in Psalm 1, for example). But this time it came in the context of Jesus' return to Jerusalem, where he would complete the Father's work and usher in the kingdom of God.

As we read of the impending judgments in an eschatological discourse (one that concerns the end times), we tend to think of ourselves as the "good guys." Few, for example, would identify themselves with the wicked servant (Matthew 24:48-49). It might be more beneficial if we came to the realization that, from time to time, we act as the good servant, but at other times we are more like the wicked servant.

Left to our own initiatives, we are not very likely to remain alert and on guard. Thanks to the death and resurrection of Jesus, however, we do have the grace to respond. As we open our lives to God's grace and daily learn to rely on that free gift, we can be alert, ready, and blessed by the Lord. He will find us "at work" when he arrives—whenever that may be. Our hope is in the promise of God and the salvation won by his Son's death and resurrection. A lack of vigilance because we presume the Lord's coming will be delayed can be dangerous; it may lead to sinful abuses. Alertness born of the sure hope that he is indeed coming will be blessed abundantly.

"Lord Jesus, we know in faith and hope that you will come again in power and majesty and judgment. We rejoice in that coming and pray that you will help us to remain always alert and faithful to your promises."

Matthew 25:1-13

¹ "Then the kingdom of heaven shall be compared to ten maidens who took their lamps and went to meet the bridegroom. ² Five of them were foolish, and five were wise. ³ For when the foolish took their lamps, they took no oil with them; ⁴ but the wise took flasks of oil with their lamps. ⁵ As the bridegroom was delayed, they all slumbered and slept. ⁶ But at midnight there was a cry, 'Behold, the bridegroom! Come out to meet him.' ⁷ Then all those maidens rose and trimmed their lamps. ⁸ And the foolish said to the wise, 'Give us some of your oil, for our lamps are going out.' ⁹ But the wise replied, 'Perhaps there will not be enough for us and for you; go rather to the dealers and buy for yourselves.' ¹⁰ And while they went to buy, the bridegroom came, and those who were ready went in with him to the marriage feast; and the door was shut. ¹¹ Afterward the other maidens came also, saying, 'Lord, lord, open to us.' ¹² But he replied, 'Truly, I say to you, I do not know you.' ¹³ Watch therefore, for you know neither the day nor the hour."

Watch therefore, for you know neither the day nor the hour.
(Matthew 25:13)

With these words from the parable of the ten bridesmaids, Jesus asked his followers to ponder his return. Are we like the five wise bridesmaids who took flasks of oil for their lamps in preparation for the great wedding feast? Or are we like the five foolish bridesmaids who took no oil with them and consequently were refused entry?

Because we live at such a frenetic pace today, we seldom take the time to reflect on one of God's wonderful promises to us as his sons and daughters—Jesus' return in glory at the end of time. If we ponder Christ's return at all, we tend to focus our thoughts on the timing and characteristics of his return, and not on the new life that awaits his faithful people.

Scripture encourages us not to be worried or concerned about the end of time. If we stand in our beliefs that we have been baptized into Jesus' death and resurrection, we can be full of hope. We can comfort one another with the truth that God wants to raise us all with Christ so that we will always be with the Lord (see 1 Thessalonians 4:17). Our belief is not in something sterile, like a set of doctrines, but in the person of Jesus, God's beloved Son. He is the personification of the biblical view of wisdom, "radiant and unfading . . . easily discerned by those who love her . . . found by those who seek her" (Wisdom 6:12). If we fix our thoughts on Jesus, he will free us from our worries and concerns and be present to us daily in our works and thoughts (see 6:15-16).

When we receive Jesus in the Eucharist, we can ask God to give us great expectation and a vibrant hope in his return. As we proclaim Jesus' death until his return in glory, we can ask the Holy Spirit to fill us with his presence, with the "oil of gladness" as we eagerly await the resurrection—the wedding feast of Jesus and his church. Before the altar, we can join the psalmist in singing, "O God, you are my God, I seek you, my soul thirsts for you . . . Because your steadfast love is better than life, my lips will praise you. So I will bless you as long as I live; I will lift up my hands and call on your name" (Psalm 63:1,3-4).

Matthew 25:14-30

14 "For it will be as when a man going on a journey called his
servants and entrusted to them his property; 15 to one he gave
five talents, to another two, to another one, to each according to
his ability. Then he went away. 16 He who had received the five
talents went at once and traded with them; and he made five
talents more. 17 So also, he who had the two talents made two
talents more. 18 But he who had received the one talent went and
dug in the ground and hid his master's money. 19 Now after a long
time the master of those servants came and settled accounts with
them. 20 And he who had received the five talents came forward,
bringing five talents more, saying, 'Master, you delivered to me
five talents; here I have made five talents more.' 21 His master
said to him, 'Well done, good and faithful servant; you have been
faithful over a little, I will set you over much; enter into the joy
of your master.' 22 And he also who had the two talents came
forward, saying, 'Master, you delivered to me two talents; here I
have made two talents more.' 23 His master said to him, 'Well
done, good and faithful servant; you have been faithful over a
little, I will set you over much; enter into the joy of your master.'
24 He also who had received the one talent came forward, saying,
'Master, I knew you to be a hard man, reaping where you did not
sow, and gathering where you did not winnow; 25 so I was afraid,
and I went and hid your talent in the ground. Here you have
what is yours.' 26 But his master answered him, 'You wicked and
slothful servant! You knew that I reap where I have not sowed,
and gather where I have not winnowed? 27 Then you ought to
have invested my money with the bankers, and at my coming I
should have received what was my own with interest. 28 So take
the talent from him, and give it to him who has the ten talents.
29 For to every one who has will more be given, and he will have

abundance; but from him who has not, even what he has will be taken away. [30] And cast the worthless servant into the outer darkness; there men will weep and gnash their teeth.' " ▨▨▨

Jesus *will* come again. We don't know when or how, but he has promised that he will return in glory to establish a new heaven and a new earth. We who live in the time between Jesus' ascension and his return are called to vigilance and resourcefulness as we await the coming of our king.

Just as an industrious wife takes initiative in caring for her household (Proverbs 31:10-31), so the church is called to manage her affairs wisely and prudently. During this time of anticipation, we are called to use our resources to spread the gospel and to ensure the spiritual prosperity of the church. We are called to serve our Master and please him in all of our actions. Our vigilance affects the way we live. By walking as "sons of light and sons of the day"—through obedience to God's commands and a life of prayer and love—we attest to our faith in Christ's return (1 Thessalonians 5:5).

Every day, we have many opportunities to use the gifts God has given us. As the parable of the talents shows, two servants took risks with the money they were given; they invested it and earned a good return. The third was afraid to take any risks, and so he hid the money and returned it to his master at the first opportunity (Matthew 25:14-30). Like the first two servants, we are also called to take risks for the kingdom of God, stepping out in faith and watching to see God move as we trust in him.

God does not give us gifts and talents so that we will hide them or turn them to selfish ends. Every one of us has been uniquely constituted by the Lord to play a role in the advancement of his kingdom, using all the resources he has given us. Whether it be money, abilities, time, or training and background, nothing is irrelevant. We can be assured that any initiatives we take to use our gifts will be blessed. Remember: God's desire for his people is always much greater than ours; he will do everything he can to bring the gospel to the ends of the earth.

As we give of ourselves, we will see God's power and glory revealed. Our active involvement in this life is truly an adventure, filled with opportunities to use all that God has given us and to see him work wonders as we do. This is our high calling. Let us accept it with gratitude and joy.

Matthew 25:31-46

[31] "When the Son of man comes in his glory, and all the angels with him, then he will sit on his glorious throne. [32] Before him will be gathered all the nations, and he will separate them one from another as a shepherd separates the sheep from the goats, [33] and he will place the sheep at his right hand, but the goats at the left. [34] Then the King will say to those at his right hand, 'Come, O blessed of my Father, inherit the kingdom prepared for you from the foundation of the world; [35] for I was hungry and you gave me food, I was thirsty and you gave me drink, I was a stranger and you welcomed me, [36] I was naked and you clothed me, I was sick and you visited me, I was in prison and you came to me.' [37] Then the righteous will answer him, 'Lord, when did we see you hungry and feed you, or thirsty and give you drink? [38] And when did we see you a stranger and welcome you, or naked and clothe you? [39] And when did we see you sick or in prison and visit you?' [40] And the King will answer them, 'Truly, I say to you, as you did it to one of the least of these my brethren, you did it to me.' [41] Then he will say to those at his left hand, 'Depart from me, you cursed, into the eternal fire prepared for the devil and his angels; [42] for I was hungry and you gave me no food, I was thirsty and you gave me no drink, [43] I was a stranger and you did not welcome me, naked and you did not clothe me, sick and in prison and you did not visit me.' [44] Then they also will answer, 'Lord, when did we see you hungry or thirsty or a stranger or naked or sick or in prison, and did not minister to you?' [45] Then he will answer them, 'Truly, I say to you, as you did it not to one of the least of these, you did it not to me.' [46] And they will go away into eternal punishment, but the righteous into eternal life."

When we read this parable, we can easily think that the "sheep"—the righteous ones—must have been naturally wonderful people! At every opportunity, it seems, they must have given of themselves for others. Truly, we feel, they deserved the eternal reward that was awaiting them.

But there is something deeper behind the story. Jesus addressed the sheep as "blessed of my Father" (Matthew 25:34). This phrase is at the heart of the difference between the sheep and the goats. The sheep sought and received the Father's blessing. They received the gift of faith because they looked to the Lord and he revealed himself to them.

Because God made himself known to them—because he bestowed on them the gift of faith—the "sheep" were able to move out of their own self-centered concerns in order to respond with love and care for the sick, the imprisoned, the hungry, and the naked. They knew that God had entered their hearts and that he would provide for all their needs. Out of a desire to see others receive this grace, they willingly gave of themselves.

The "goats," on the other hand, didn't open themselves to receive God's overflowing gift of love. They didn't believe that the Father wanted to bless them abundantly. Consequently, they were too concerned for their own welfare—their own status and prestige—to look beyond themselves and bring God's love and compassion to others. Thus blinded to the grace of God, thinking only of themselves, they were dispatched to the same darkness in which they had lived, now revealed in its fullness.

God wants us to turn to him, to know that he reveals himself to everyone who seeks him sincerely (see Hebrews 11:6). It is only through faith in God (which draws us to his love) that we can reach out to people effectively. When we try to do it out of our own goodness or will power, we become like a dry spring from which no life can flow to others. If, on the other hand, we ground ourselves in God's love and salvation, we will be able to give and serve selflessly.

"Father, we know we need your grace to serve others. Help us seek you above all things and to care for others only out of your love."

The Cross of Christ

An Overview of Matthew's Passion
by Gregory Roa

MATTHEW
26–27

Matthew 26:1-75

1   When Jesus had finished all these sayings, he said to his disciples, 2 "You know that after two days the Passover is coming, and the Son of man will be delivered up to be crucified."
3   Then the chief priests and the elders of the people gathered in the palace of the high priest, who was called Caiaphas, 4 and took counsel together in order to arrest Jesus by stealth and kill him. 5 But they said, "Not during the feast, lest there be a tumult among the people."
6   Now when Jesus was at Bethany in the house of Simon the leper, 7 a woman came up to him with an alabaster flask of very expensive ointment, and she poured it on his head, as he sat at table. 8 But when the disciples saw it, they were indignant, saying, "Why this waste? 9 For this ointment might have been sold for a large sum, and given to the poor." 10 But Jesus, aware of this, said to them, "Why do you trouble the woman? For she has done a beautiful thing to me. 11 For you always have the poor with you, but you will not always have me. 12 In pouring this ointment on my body she has done it to prepare me for burial. 13 Truly, I say to you, wherever this gospel is preached in the whole world, what she has done will be told in memory of her."
14   Then one of the twelve, who was called Judas Iscariot, went to the chief priests 15 and said, "What will you give me if I deliver him to you?" And they paid him thirty pieces of silver. 16 And from that moment he sought an opportunity to betray him.
17   Now on the first day of Unleavened Bread the disciples came to Jesus, saying, "Where will you have us prepare for you to eat the passover?" 18 He said, "Go into the city to a certain one, and say to him, 'The Teacher says, My time is at hand; I will keep the passover at your house with my disciples.' " 19 And the disciples did as Jesus had directed them, and they prepared the passover.

²⁰ When it was evening, he sat at table with the twelve disciples; ²¹ and as they were eating, he said, "Truly, I say to you, one of you will betray me." ²² And they were very sorrowful, and began to say to him one after another, "Is it I, Lord?" ²³ He answered, "He who has dipped his hand in the dish with me, will betray me. ²⁴ The Son of man goes as it is written of him, but woe to that man by whom the Son of man is betrayed! It would have been better for that man if he had not been born." ²⁵ Judas, who betrayed him, said, "Is it I, Master?" He said to him, "You have said so."
²⁶ Now as they were eating, Jesus took bread, and blessed, and broke it, and gave it to the disciples and said, "Take, eat; this is my body." ²⁷ And he took a cup, and when he had given thanks he gave it to them, saying, "Drink of it, all of you; ²⁸ for this is my blood of the covenant, which is poured out for many for the forgiveness of sins. ²⁹ I tell you I shall not drink again of this fruit of the vine until that day when I drink it new with you in my Father's kingdom."
³⁰ And when they had sung a hymn, they went out to the Mount of Olives. ³¹ Then Jesus said to them, "You will all fall away because of me this night; for it is written, 'I will strike the shepherd, and the sheep of the flock will be scattered.' ³² But after I am raised up, I will go before you to Galilee." ³³ Peter declared to him, "Though they all fall away because of you, I will never fall away." ³⁴ Jesus said to him, "Truly, I say to you, this very night, before the cock crows, you will deny me three times." ³⁵ Peter said to him, "Even if I must die with you, I will not deny you." And so said all the disciples. ³⁶ Then Jesus went with them to a place called Gethsemane, and he said to his disciples, "Sit here, while I go yonder and pray." ³⁷ And taking with him Peter and the two sons of Zebedee, he began to be sorrowful and troubled. ³⁸ Then he said to them, "My soul is very sorrowful, even to death; remain here, and watch with me." ³⁹ And going a little farther he fell on his face and prayed, "My Father, if it be possible, let this cup pass from me; nevertheless, not as I will, but as

thou wilt." [40] And he came to the disciples and found them sleeping; and he said to Peter, "So, could you not watch with me one hour? [41] Watch and pray that you may not enter into temptation; the spirit indeed is willing, but the flesh is weak." [42] Again, for the second time, he went away and prayed, "My Father, if this cannot pass unless I drink it, thy will be done." [43] And again he came and found them sleeping, for their eyes were heavy. [44] So, leaving them again, he went away and prayed for the third time, saying the same words. [45] Then he came to the disciples and said to them, "Are you still sleeping and taking your rest? Behold, the hour is at hand, and the Son of man is betrayed into the hands of sinners. [46] Rise, let us be going; see, my betrayer is at hand."

[47] While he was still speaking, Judas came, one of the twelve, and with him a great crowd with swords and clubs, from the chief priests and the elders of the people. [48] Now the betrayer had given them a sign, saying, "The one I shall kiss is the man; seize him." [49] And he came up to Jesus at once and said, "Hail, Master!" And he kissed him. [50] Jesus said to him, "Friend, why are you here?" Then they came up and laid hands on Jesus and seized him. [51] And behold, one of those who were with Jesus stretched out his hand and drew his sword, and struck the slave of the high priest, and cut off his ear. [52] Then Jesus said to him, "Put your sword back into its place; for all who take the sword will perish by the sword. [53] Do you think that I cannot appeal to my Father, and he will at once send me more than twelve legions of angels? [54] But how then should the scriptures be fulfilled, that it must be so?" [55] At that hour Jesus said to the crowds, "Have you come out as against a robber, with swords and clubs to capture me? Day after day I sat in the temple teaching, and you did not seize me. [56] But all this has taken place, that the scriptures of the prophets might be fulfilled." Then all the disciples forsook him and fled.

[57] Then those who had seized Jesus led him to Caiaphas the high

priest, where the scribes and the elders had gathered. [58] But Peter followed him at a distance, as far as the courtyard of the high priest, and going inside he sat with the guards to see the end. [59] Now the chief priests and the whole council sought false testimony against Jesus that they might put him to death, [60] but they found none, though many false witnesses came forward. At last two came forward [61] and said, "This fellow said, 'I am able to destroy the temple of God, and to build it in three days.' " [62] And the high priest stood up and said, "Have you no answer to make? What is it that these men testify against you?" [63] But Jesus was silent. And the high priest said to him, "I adjure you by the living God, tell us if you are the Christ, the Son of God." [64] Jesus said to him, "You have said so. But I tell you, hereafter you will see the Son of man seated at the right hand of Power, and coming on the clouds of heaven."
[65] Then the high priest tore his robes, and said, "He has uttered blasphemy. Why do we still need witnesses? You have now heard his blasphemy. [66] What is your judgment?" They answered, "He deserves death." [67] Then they spat in his face, and struck him; and some slapped him, [68] saying, "Prophesy to us, you Christ! Who is it that struck you?"
[69] Now Peter was sitting outside in the courtyard. And a maid came up to him, and said, "You also were with Jesus the Galilean." [70] But he denied it before them all, saying, "I do not know what you mean." [71] And when he went out to the porch, another maid saw him, and she said to the bystanders, "This man was with Jesus of Nazareth." [72] And again he denied it with an oath, "I do not know the man." [73] After a little while the bystanders came up and said to Peter, "Certainly you are also one of them, for your accent betrays you." [74] Then he began to invoke a curse on himself and to swear, "I do not know the man." And immediately the cock crowed. [75] And Peter remembered the saying of Jesus, "Before the cock crows, you will deny me three times." And he went out and wept bitterly. 🌸🌸🌸

Matthew 27:1-66

[1] When morning came, all the chief priests and the elders of the people took counsel against Jesus to put him to death; [2] and they bound him and led him away and delivered him to Pilate the governor.

[3] When Judas, his betrayer, saw that he was condemned, he repented and brought back the thirty pieces of silver to the chief priests and the elders, [4] saying, "I have sinned in betraying innocent blood." They said, "What is that to us? See to it yourself." [5] And throwing down the pieces of silver in the temple, he departed; and he went and hanged himself. [6] But the chief priests, taking the pieces of silver, said, "It is not lawful to put them into the treasury, since they are blood money." [7] So they took counsel, and bought with them the potter's field, to bury strangers in. [8] Therefore that field has been called the Field of Blood to this day. [9] Then was fulfilled what had been spoken by the prophet Jeremiah, saying, "And they took the thirty pieces of silver, the price of him on whom a price had been set by some of the sons of Israel, [10] and they gave them for the potter's field, as the Lord directed me." [11] Now Jesus stood before the governor; and the governor asked him, "Are you the King of the Jews?" Jesus said, "You have said so." [12] But when he was accused by the chief priests and elders, he made no answer. [13] Then Pilate said to him, "Do you not hear how many things they testify against you?" [14] But he gave him no answer, not even to a single charge; so that the governor wondered greatly. [15] Now at the feast the governor was accustomed to release for the crowd any one prisoner whom they wanted. [16] And they had then a notorious prisoner, called Barabbas. [17] So when they had gathered, Pilate said to them, "Whom do you want me to release for you, Barabbas or Jesus who is called Christ?" [18] For he knew that it was out of envy that they had delivered him up. [19] Besides, while he

was sitting on the judgment seat, his wife sent word to him, "Have nothing to do with that righteous man, for I have suffered much over him today in a dream." [20] Now the chief priests and the elders persuaded the people to ask for Barabbas and destroy Jesus. [21] The governor again said to them, "Which of the two do you want me to release for you?" And they said, "Barabbas." [22] Pilate said to them, "Then what shall I do with Jesus who is called Christ?" They all said, "Let him be crucified." [23] And he said, "Why, what evil has he done?" But they shouted all the more, "Let him be crucified." [24] So when Pilate saw that he was gaining nothing, but rather that a riot was beginning, he took water and washed his hands before the crowd, saying, "I am innocent of this righteous man's blood; see to it yourselves." [25] And all the people answered, "His blood be on us and on our children!" [26] Then he released for them Barabbas, and having scourged Jesus, delivered him to be crucified. [27] Then the soldiers of the governor took Jesus into the praetorium, and they gathered the whole battalion before him. [28] And they stripped him and put a scarlet robe upon him, [29] and plaiting a crown of thorns they put it on his head, and put a reed in his right hand. And kneeling before him they mocked him, saying, "Hail, King of the Jews!" [30] And they spat upon him, and took the reed and struck him on the head. [31] And when they had mocked him, they stripped him of the robe, and put his own clothes on him, and led him away to crucify him. [32] As they went out, they came upon a man of Cyrene, Simon by name; this man they compelled to carry his cross. [33] And when they came to a place called Golgotha (which means the place of a skull), [34] they offered him wine to drink, mingled with gall; but when he tasted it, he would not drink it. [35] And when they had crucified him, they divided his garments among them by casting lots; [36] then they sat down and kept watch over him there. [37] And over his head they put the charge against him, which read, "This is Jesus the King of the Jews." [38] Then two robbers were crucified with him, one on the right and one on the left. [39] And those who passed by derided him, wagging their heads [40] and saying, "You who would destroy the temple and build it in three days, save yourself! If you are the Son of God, come down from the cross." [41] So also the chief priests, with the scribes and elders, mocked him, saying, [42] "He saved others; he cannot save himself. He is the King of Israel; let him come down now from the cross, and we will believe in him. [43] He trusts in God; let God deliver him now, if he desires him; for he said, 'I am the Son of God.'" [44] And the robbers who were crucified with him also reviled him in the same way.

[45] Now from the sixth hour there was darkness over all the land until the ninth hour. [46] And about the ninth hour Jesus cried with a loud voice, "Eli, Eli, lama sabachthani?" that is, "My God, my God, why hast thou forsaken me?" [47] And some of the bystanders hearing it said, "This man is calling Elijah." [48] And one of them at once ran and took a sponge, filled it with vinegar, and put it on a reed, and gave it to him to drink. [49] But the others said, "Wait, let us see whether Elijah will come to save him." [50] And Jesus cried again with a loud voice and yielded up his spirit.

[51] And behold, the curtain of the temple was torn in two, from top to bottom; and the earth shook, and the rocks were split; [52] the tombs also were opened, and many bodies of the saints who had fallen asleep were raised, [53] and coming out of the tombs after his resurrection they went into the holy city and appeared to many. [54] When the centurion and those who were with him, keeping watch over Jesus, saw the earthquake and what took place, they were filled with awe, and said, "Truly this was the Son of God!"

[55] There were also many women there, looking on from afar, who had followed Jesus from Galilee, ministering to him; [56] among whom were Mary Magdalene, and Mary the mother of James and Joseph, and the mother of the sons of Zebedee.

[57] When it was evening, there came a rich man from Arimathea, named Joseph, who also was a disciple of Jesus. [58] He went to Pilate and asked for the body of Jesus. Then Pilate ordered it to be given to him. [59] And Joseph took the body, and wrapped it in a clean linen shroud, [60] and laid it in his own new tomb, which he had hewn in the rock; and he rolled a great stone to the door of the tomb, and departed. [61] Mary Magdalene and the other Mary were there, sitting opposite the sepulchre.

[62] Next day, that is, after the day of Preparation, the chief priests and the Pharisees gathered before Pilate [63] and said, "Sir, we remember how that impostor said, while he was still alive, 'After three days I will rise again.' [64] Therefore order the sepulchre to be made secure until the third day, lest his disciples go and steal him away, and tell the people, 'He has risen from the dead,' and the last fraud will be worse than the first." [65] Pilate said to them, "You have a guard of soldiers; go, make it as secure as you can." [66] So they went and made the sepulchre secure by sealing the stone and setting a guard.

I magine that you are a non-Christian seeing a copy of the gospels for the very first time. Not knowing anything about Christianity, at just a glance, you would probably notice an odd thing about these writings: In each gospel, more detail is supplied about Jesus' final hours than about any other event in his life. Immediately, you ask: "What was so significant about this person's death? Why would it overshadow all the good things he said and did during his life?"

None of the gospels was written in a vacuum; each of them grew out of a community of believers seeking to deepen their faith and love for Jesus, whose death and resurrection had transformed their lives. Consequently, while the sacred authors did reveal the importance of Jesus' sayings and miracles, they maintained a primary focus on his passion, crucifixion, and death, because in these events they saw the principal work of our salvation. Without Jesus' cross, all his words and deeds would lose their power and meaning.

Matthew's Focus

This broad, over-arching theme of Jesus' cross and resurrection served as the keystone of Matthew's narrative. Matthew wrote for a Jewish community who had converted to Christianity, and, like all Jews in the late first century, these Jewish Christians keenly felt the impact of the dramatic events of their time—the destruction of the Temple and the continuing Roman occupation in their homeland. Yet, these new Christian converts in Matthew's community felt doubly outcast: They were also being driven out of the Jewish synagogues for their belief in Jesus.

The pain of rejection was only part of the struggle of Matthew's community. Their own newly born church was witnessing an influx of non-Jewish converts. For the first time, Jews found themselves worshipping and living alongside Gentiles who accepted the gospel, but knew nothing of the Torah. The pressure to accept this new reality must have been great.

Besieged by outside forces, and straining with tension from within, Matthew's community was in upheaval. It was to this situation that Matthew proclaimed the word of truth, speaking of things that were important to his audience's circumstances. By examining some key elements in Matthew's passion narrative, we can appreciate the community for which Matthew wrote and gain a deeper understanding of Jesus' victory on the cross as it applies to our lives today.

Fulfilling God's Promises

From the outset, Matthew's passion narrative reveals Jesus as a Messiah who remains in control of the events leading to his arrest and death. Matthew begins his story with a matter-of-fact declaration by Jesus: "You know that after two days the Passover is coming, and the Son of man will be delivered up to be crucified" (Matthew 26:2). The tone was set: a difficult trial was to face Jesus, but he would embrace the struggle decisively, confident because he was doing his Father's will.

From this point on, Matthew showed Jesus as the obedient Son of God, fulfilling his Father's plan in all things. Just as Jesus had earlier told John the Baptist that he must "fulfill all righteousness" (Matthew 3:15), so here, at the end of his ministry, Jesus fulfilled God's will, moving forward readily to his trial and death. In this way, Matthew showed Jesus living out the teaching he gave his disciples: "Seek first his kingdom and his righteousness" (6:33). Ever faithful to God, Jesus showed himself to be the "beloved Son" in whom his Father was "well pleased" (3:17).

For Matthew, Jesus' radical obedience to God revealed him to

be the true and long-awaited Messiah. Immediately after recounting Jesus' passion prediction, Matthew tells of his anointing at
Bethany (Matthew 26:6-13). The Greek word *Christos* means *the
anointed one* and, though the disciples protested the exorbitant
waste of precious oil, Jesus accepted it as a "beautiful thing"
(26:10), which prepared him "for burial" (26:12). It is significant
that a woman anointed Jesus, not one of his own disciples. Though
the Jews were God's chosen people, they had failed to recognize the
Messiah in their midst. In contrast, the Gentiles, "sinners," and
women—outsiders like those gaining prominence in Matthew's
community—rushed to accept him as Savior. For Jesus, discipleship
did not depend on gender, background, or race. True disciples are
those who, like the anonymous woman at Bethany, have faith in
Jesus and do the will of God (see 12:50).

Throughout his passion narrative, Matthew leads us through
scriptural allusions and prophecies fulfilled by Jesus' death—all
signs of Jesus' obedience to his Father's plan. As you read through
Matthew's passion narrative, see how many of these Old Testament
parallels you can find: Psalm 2:1-2; Psalm 22; Psalm 41:9; Isaiah
53:3,7; Jeremiah 32:6-9; Zechariah 11:12-13; 13:7. So much did
Matthew rely on the Hebrew scriptures to explain why Jesus had to
die that even Jesus' final words are a direct quote: "Eli, Eli, lama
sabachthani?" that is, "My God, my God, why have you forsaken
me?" (Matthew 27:46; see Psalm 22:1).

Embracing the "Hour" of the Cross

By using so many scriptural allusions, Matthew was able to
accomplish two major goals. First, he could reassure the Jewish
Christians that Jesus truly had to die to fulfill the Father's plan for
us; the Messiah *had* to be rejected in order to save his people.
Second, and more significantly, the scriptural parallels reveal

that, despite the upheaval, chaos, and pain of the passion, God was, in fact, in control throughout these awful events. When Jesus proclaimed: "My time is at hand; I will keep the passover" (Matthew 26:18), Matthew used the Greek term *kairos*, meaning *hour* or *moment*. Jesus repeated this at Gethsemane when he was arrested: "Behold, the hour is at hand" (26:45). However it may have appeared to the chief priests and scribes, Jesus decisively embraced the passion as the very moment for which he had been preparing his whole life.

Jesus' suffering was no "accident" or "twist of fate." It was not even the by-product of the chief priests' opposition, Judas' betrayal, or Pilate's power. Jesus' death was God's will for the salvation of all humankind. Still, Matthew made no attempt to hide the emotional turmoil this decision caused Jesus. In fact, he depicted the real, human sorrow and anguish evident when Jesus prayed: "My Father, if it be possible, let this cup pass from me" (Matthew 26:39).

Jesus did not shrink back from the anguish of his cross. He endured it to win our salvation. Now, Matthew's community, undergoing upheaval and suffering, was also encouraged to follow the way of the cross. Despite appearances, God was still in control over history, even over the oppression and tension they were experiencing. It was just as Jesus had promised them: "If any man would come after me, let him deny himself and take up his cross and follow me. For whoever would save his life will lose it, and whoever loses his life for my sake will find it" (Matthew 16:24-25).

Inaugurating a New World

For the Christian Jews and Gentile converts in Matthew's community, Jesus' coming "to fulfill" the "law and the prophets" (Matthew 5:17) meant the dynamic arrival of a new stage of history. Like a new Moses, Jesus had already superseded the law and the prophets in his Sermon on the Mount (5:1–7:29). Now, at the Last Supper, he instituted a new covenant, which more than surpassed Israel's former relationship with Yahweh. Matthew depicted this meal as a Passover *seder*, evoking a rich imagery for his Jewish readers. Employing the same symbols the Jews had used since Moses' time, Jesus did more than recall Israel's redemption from slavery. He *transformed* the ceremony, saying: "Take, eat; this is my body. . . . This is my blood of the covenant, which is poured out for many for the forgiveness of sins" (26:26,28). The Son of God sacrificed his body and blood to create a new Israel, a church that included Jews and Gentiles, women and men, and every marginalized soul who appears in various places in Matthew's gospel. Through Christ, all now have access to Jesus' *Abba*—our Father.

At the end of the Last Supper, Jesus told his disciples: "I shall not drink again of this fruit of the vine until that day when I drink it new with you in my Father's kingdom" (Matthew 26:29). This statement—which is probably as close to the exact words of Jesus as any saying we find in the gospels—indicates, again, Jesus' awareness of his fate and his willingness to move forward to the victory he would achieve in the cross. It also made Matthew's readers aware that they could no longer look back to the Mosaic laws and rituals from which they came. Because Jesus' time had come, all Christians could now drink the wine of the new covenant, a wine that could not be contained by the old wineskins (see 9:17).

This new stage of history began at the very moment of Jesus' death, as Matthew showed with the events that occurred immediately thereafter:

> Now, from the sixth hour there was darkness over all the land . . . and Jesus cried again with a loud voice and yielded up his spirit. And behold, the curtain of the temple was

torn in two, from top to bottom; and the earth shook, and the rocks were split; the tombs also were opened, and many bodies of the saints who had fallen asleep were raised. . . . When the centurion and those who were with him, keeping watch over Jesus, saw the earthquake and what took place, they were filled with awe and said, "Truly this was the Son of God!" (Matthew 27:45,50-54)

Jesus' death accomplished the very thing that Judaism looked for with the coming of the Messiah: the new era of the reign of God, when he promised to shake the earth and raise up his holy ones. Our salvation and renewal began when Jesus died on the cross. Yet, God's chosen people—even Jesus' own disciples—missed its inauguration. Once again, it was a group of outsiders, the Roman soldiers, who readily accepted the cross and the signs of transformation that accompanied it.

Hope and Challenge

By telling the story of Jesus' death and resurrection as he did, Matthew sought to hold out hope to a community undergoing enormous pressures from inside and out. On a personal level, we all experience struggles: the pain of rejection, the challenge to do God's will in the face of opposition, the sorrow of apparent failures that face us every day. Like Matthew's community, we, too, can learn that not every obstacle comes from outside of ourselves: "The spirit indeed is willing, but the flesh is weak" (Matthew 26:41). Growth and renewal come at a price: opening ourselves to be shaken up and allowing the Spirit to breathe life into us.

The message of the passion is that Jesus is with us in this process of the upheaval of our old life. Matthew's term for earthquake—*seismos*—was the same word he used when Jesus saved the disciples by calming the *seismos* (*great storm*) on the lake (Matthew 8:23-27). Jesus remains with us, in control of our history, just as he was on the lake and during the distressing events of the passion. While it is a challenge to follow the way of the cross, it is, at the same time, our best hope. If we understand anything from praying through Matthew's narrative, it is that Jesus has already won the victory. We do not see its fullness, but neither could Jesus' disciples—or Matthew's community. Let us be confident that we walk in the new day of God's righteousness and that, with those who persevere with joy, we will "see the Son of man seated at the right hand of Power, and coming on the clouds of heaven" (26:64).

A DEVOTIONAL COMMENTARY ON MATTHEW

With Jesus in the Holy Land

Fr. Joseph A. Mindling, O.F.M. Cap.

Among the greatest treasures bequeathed to us by the authors of the New Testament are their descriptions of the last days of Jesus' public ministry, climaxing in his brutal execution and his triumphant victory over death. The sections that recount this high point of our Lord's earthly mission in the four gospels are called the passion and resurrection narratives (Matthew 26–28; Mark 14–16; Luke 22–24; John 18–21).

For those who live outside the Holy Land, it is customary to see our Lord as an isolated object of religious devotion—a statue of the risen Christ or a crucifix on a rosary. The locations in which the events of the passion took place can seem like secondary—almost superfluous—backdrop. Yet for those who were Jesus' companions, the actual places where each event at the end of the Master's life took place added significance to what he did—the colonnaded outer porches of the temple, the barracks where Roman soldiers tortured prisoners, the dusty narrow streets of Jerusalem, the City of David (John 10:22-39; Mark 15:1-20).

Jesus invited us to take up our cross and walk behind him (Mark 8:34). One approach that can help us to follow in our Redeemer's footsteps is to focus on some of those physical sites where he demonstrated his love for us most tangibly. This is hardly a new idea; it has served generations of believers. It is the inspiration that has motivated pilgrims to journey to the Holy Land throughout the centuries. It is the insight that generated the practice of making the Stations of the Cross. For a few minutes, let us re-appropriate this tradition as well, pondering some of what we know about those places that Jesus sanctified by making them part of our salvation history.

The Temple. All four gospels describe our Lord preaching, debating, and performing healings in the temple in the days leading up to his arrest. This grand edifice, still being embellished by artisans as part of Herod's remodeling, was the most impressive Jewish place of worship in the world. Comparable in size and beauty to the marble monuments of the Greeks and the Romans, it was also considered the holiest spot on earth. Its glistening facade of white marble and gold represented the presence of divine glory among the people. Its clouds of sacrificial smoke and rising choruses of praise symbolized the reverence that Israel owed to the God of the covenant. Yet Jesus spoke of his own body as the prototypical temple that would rise up, even as the walls of the old sanctuary would fall, never to rise again. Through the Paschal Mystery, Jesus transforms us into temples of the New Covenant (John 2:13-25; see 1 Corinthians 6:19).

The Cenacle. Christian tradition places the site of the Last Supper in a section of Jerusalem—on the southwestern ridge of the city—where well-to-do priestly families resided, well cared for by their domestics. Jesus obviously picked an upper room "in the right neighborhood" to officiate as High Priest of the new covenant and to wash his friends' feet as servant of the servants of God. Ironically, this same "respectable" quarter of the city, the area medieval pilgrims called Mount Zion, was where many believe the priest Annas lived, and where Jesus was brought back for secret, illegal interrogations (Luke 22:7-13; Matthew 26:57-68).

The Mount of Olives. The agony Jesus suffered in the garden prior to his arrest is remembered today on the eastern side of Jerusalem in a shrine church near the bottom of a slope, much of which is covered by Jewish cemeteries and olive trees, some of them very ancient. This area has maintained its popularity as a burial place in part because it is identified with the Valley of Jehoshaphat, which the book of Joel associates with an apocalyptic conclusion to history as we know it (Joel 3:2,12,14). The name Gethsemane, meaning oil press, has suggested to Christian artists the presence of a gnarled and leafy orchard, lending seclusion and greater darkness to the hillside in the late evening. Imagine Jesus slipping away from the hustle and heat of the city to find time here to collect his thoughts and pray. How appropriate that the Conqueror of Death should engage the enemy in a place dotted with so many monuments to seemingly invincible mortality (Luke 22:39-53; Mark 14:32-52).

The Courtrooms. The evangelists tell us of Jesus' being arraigned before the High Priests Annas and Caiaphas, the Sanhedrin, King Herod, and Pontius Pilate. Archeological remains and ancient written descriptions suggest that the atmosphere in Palestinian courtrooms would have had much in common with judicial proceedings under any dictatorship. The gospel accounts reflect the trappings of bureaucracy and politically determined outcomes carried out in solemn, official surroundings: officious personnel, posturing judges, and an innocent defendant accepting the inevitability of a guilty verdict. Bystanders howl out their hostility, or worse, look on in silence (Mark 14:53–15:15; John 18:12–19:16).

Golgotha. After being unjustly sentenced to public execution, Jesus was humiliated by being paraded through the narrow, crowded streets of a city busy preparing for the most important feast of the year. Many of the foreign visitors would have considered the whole business of the Nazarene's crucifixion an unwelcome intrusion into their high holy day festivities.

Jesus' cross and those of the criminals executed with him were raised on a mound in a basin-like depression, the site of a long-abandoned stone quarry. Christ, marginalized by the religious establishment, was raised up on a natural pedestal, a stone, which the construction workers had rejected and which reminded the popular imagination of a skull (Matthew 21:42; Psalm 118:22).

Not far from this outcropping, certain individuals had paid dearly to have burial chambers carved into the sloping walls of the quarry. Minor landscaping changes had lent an air of respectability to a resting place for the wealthy, conveniently (and legally) located just outside the city walls. How tempting it must have been for the Roman occupation authorities to insult the Jewish populace by using this hallowed spot for the execution of controversial criminals! It is no wonder, too, that Mary Magdalene presumed that anyone out early on the first working day of the week would be part of the gardening clean-up staff (Luke 23:26-56; John 19:17-42).

Because of the natural human aversion to psychological and physical pain, successive retelling of what happened during Jesus' final days might well have tended to abbreviate the accounts of our Lord's suffering and to expand the reports of his successes and later vindication. However, the Christian community obviously recognized from the beginning the great spiritual value of revisiting the saving events of the first Christian Passover. Instead of letting this sacred memory fade, the Spirit moved the writers and readers of the New Testament to preserve these sacred moments. The same Holy Spirit has enabled Christian people in every age and place to understand the narratives of Jesus' pain and victory as living springs of spiritual strength and inspiration. Western painters and eastern iconographers, liturgists and hymn writers, mystics and penitents—we all draw on these chapters to experience what Jesus meant when he prophesied: "When I am lifted up, I will draw everyone to myself" (John 12:32).

The Resurrection

MATTHEW
28

Matthew 28:1-15

[1] Now after the sabbath, toward the dawn of the first day of the week, Mary Magdalene and the other Mary went to see the sepulchre. [2] And behold, there was a great earthquake; for an angel of the Lord descended from heaven and came and rolled back the stone, and sat upon it. [3] His appearance was like lightning, and his raiment white as snow. [4] And for fear of him the guards trembled and became like dead men. [5] But the angel said to the women, "Do not be afraid; for I know that you seek Jesus who was crucified. [6] He is not here; for he has risen, as he said. Come, see the place where he lay. [7] Then go quickly and tell his disciples that he has risen from the dead, and behold, he is going before you to Galilee; there you will see him. Lo, I have told you." [8] So they departed quickly from the tomb with fear and great joy, and ran to tell his disciples. [9] And behold, Jesus met them and said, "Hail!" And they came up and took hold of his feet and worshipped him. [10] Then Jesus said to them, "Do not be afraid; go and tell my brethren to go to Galilee, and there they will see me."

[11] While they were going, behold, some of the guard went into the city and told the chief priests all that had taken place. [12] And when they had assembled with the elders and taken counsel, they gave a sum of money to the soldiers [13] and said, "Tell people, 'His disciples came by night and stole him away while we were asleep.' [14] And if this comes to the governor's ears, we will satisfy him and keep you out of trouble." [15] So they took the money and did as they were directed; and this story has been spread among the Jews to this day.

The women had come to pay their last respects to the teacher who had changed their lives. It was dawn on the first day of the week when they came to the tomb. Matthew's account does not tell us why they came; perhaps they planned to hold a day-long vigil there.

What perhaps started as a pious excursion, however, was soon changed. God's presence became evident—Matthew wrote of an earthquake and an angel who rolled the stone from in front of Jesus' tomb (Matthew 28:2). The angel instructed the women to tell the apostles what they had seen and heard. Afraid, yet filled with joy (28:8), the two Marys ran to the disciples to proclaim Jesus' resurrection from the dead.

The women were joyful because they had just seen the risen Lord. At the same time, they were fearful, in part because they had been called to proclaim a truth that they knew might be rejected. Their response was not unlike our own when we experience the wonder of God, but are hesitant to speak of it for fear of what people might think. Despite their concern, the women carried out the angel's instruction because the work of God in them was greater than their fear.

The story of the two women shows how much impact a simple honest witness can have. The Jewish priests and elders had concocted a story to explain away the resurrection of Jesus (Matthew 28:12-15). One might suspect that the story of the religious officials would be more credible than the word of two simple Jewish women (especially since their testimony could be discounted under rabbinic law). Indeed, we might wonder why Jesus did not pick someone who could better shape the popular opinions of the day.

God had a better plan, and the two women were part of it. The testimony of the two Marys—and that of all the other witnesses to the truth of Jesus—won the day. Christianity outlived the Roman empire—and every empire since—all because witnesses to the truth like these two women have responded to God and faithfully proclaimed what they have seen.

"Lord Jesus, give us the courage to follow the Spirit's lead, and to share your work in us. May the joy of advancing your kingdom overcome our fear, shyness, lack of confidence, or expectations of rejection. Help us to share your love."

Matthew 28:16-20

16 Now the eleven disciples went to Galilee, to the mountain to which Jesus had directed them. 17 And when they saw him they worshipped him; but some doubted. 18 And Jesus came and said to them, "All authority in heaven and on earth has been given to me. 19 Go therefore and make disciples of all nations, baptizing them in the name of the Father and of the Son and of the Holy Spirit, 20 teaching them to observe all that I have commanded you; and lo, I am with you always, to the close of the age."

"Go therefore and make disciples of all nations, baptizing them in the name of the Father and of the Son and of the Holy Spirit."
(Matthew 28:19)

These words of Jesus are known as the "Great Commission." We can view them as his final "marching orders" to the eleven disciples who had been his companions for the past three years. These disciples were now commanded to bring the message of new life to the whole world. Fortunately for us, with the grace of the Holy Spirit upon them, they were able to carry out this commission.

But these words were not meant to apply just to only eleven men on a mountain. Christianity has flourished throughout two millennia because others took seriously this great commission of Jesus. We, too, have been commissioned by Jesus to "make disciples of all nations."

What a daunting task! How often we shrink from it, fearful lest we offend someone or lead them to think we are hopelessly out of touch with the world. Yet Jesus ended his commission with the comforting words: "I am with you always, to the close of the age" (Matthew 28:20). We can stand on this promise. He will be with us as we carry out his commission. He will help us to overcome fear, pride, or anything else that deters us from preaching his word.

Through baptism, Jesus lives in us. He who died for us has given us new life, and we can rejoice now and in heaven when we share that life with others. There are many ways we can do this. We can feed the hungry, comfort the lonely, visit the sick. We can work to correct injustice in our societies. We can build strong, loving families. We can invite people to our churches. In all these ways, we bear witness to a loving God who has provided his creatures with ways to share in his divine goodness. In all these ways, we build God's kingdom on earth.

"Lord Jesus, thank you for your apostles and for all your people throughout the centuries who have carried out your mandate to spread the gospel. Give us the grace to be among those who continue to carry out your great commission. We know that you will be with us always."

A DEVOTIONAL COMMENTARY ON MATTHEW

Topical Index of Matthew's Gospel

Events in the Life of Jesus:

Healings:

Miracles of Jesus:

Parables of Jesus:

Teachings and Sayings of Jesus:

The New Testament Devotional Commentary Series
From The Word Among Us Press

Enjoy praying through the Gospels with these faith-filled commentaries.
Each commentary includes the complete Scripture text, followed by a devotional meditation based on the passage—over 600 inspirational meditations in the series!

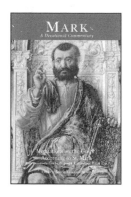
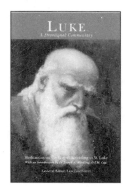

Also available:

Experience the Holy Spirit as you read Acts of the Apostles.

Journey with St. Paul as he preaches to the Romans and Galatians.

To Order call 1-800-775-9673
or order online at www.wordamongus.org